EP Zoology Printables: Levels 1-4

This book belongs to:

_____

This book was made for your convenience. It is available for printing from the Easy Peasy All-in-One Homeschool website. It contains all of the printables from Easy Peasy's zoology course. The instructions for each page are found in the online course.

Easy Peasy All-in-One Homeschool is a free online homeschool curriculum providing high quality education for children around the globe. It provides complete courses for preschool through high school graduation. For EP's curriculum visit allinonehomeschool.com.

EP Zoology Printables: Levels 1-4

ISBN: 9798640334159

First Edition: June 2020

Sort

Cut out the various animal cards and sort them based on whether they lay eggs (oviparous) or give birth to live young (viviparous).

frog	ape	bear	flamingo
grasshopper	alligator	pig	dove
raccoon	snake	rabbit	platypus
duck	elephant	tortoise	stork

(This page left intentionally blank)

Oviparous (lay eggs)

Viviparous (live young)

(This page left intentionally blank)

Animal

Classification

Lapbook

(This page left intentionally blank)

Classifying Living Things

Cut out the rectangle as one piece and fold on the dotted line. Inside (opposite the "glue here" side), write the divisions of taxonomy in order from biggest to smallest: kingdom, phylum, class, order, family, genus, species. If you're going to glue your lapbook to a file folder or poster board you can do that now or wait until you've completed all of the pieces.

(glue here)

Classifying living things

(This page left intentionally blank)

Invertebrates

Cut out the rectangle as one piece. Fold the left side in (on the line at **A**), and fold the right side in (on the line at **B**). Cut on the dotted lines so that 1, 2, 3, and 4 are strips you can open to the fold. On the inside (opposite "glue here"), write the four main classes of invertebrates.: echinoderms, annelids, mollusks, and arthropods.

1

2

3

4

↑ A

(glue here)

↓ B

Four Main Invertebrate Classes

(This page left intentionally blank)

Vertebrates

Cut out the rectangle as one piece. Fold the left side in (on the line at **A**), and fold the right side in (on the line at **B**). Cut on the dotted lines so that 1, 2, 3, and 4 are strips you can open to the fold. On the inside (opposite "glue here"), write the five classes of vertebrates: mammals, reptiles, amphibians, birds, and fish.

1	
2	
3	
4	
5	

↑ A

(glue here)

B ↓

Five Main Vertebrate Classes

(This page left intentionally blank)

Invertebrates and Vertebrates

Cut out the rectangle as one piece and fold on the center line. Cut on the dotted line to the center fold. Inside (opposite the "glue here" side), write vertebrate and invertebrate under the correct flap.

(glue here)

Has a backbone

Does not have a backbone

(This page left intentionally blank)

Reptiles and Fish

Cut out the rectangles and fold on the dotted line. Inside (opposite the "glue here" side), write characteristics of reptiles (dry skin or scales, breathe air, lay eggs) and fish (fins, tail, scales, use gills to breathe underwater).

(glue here)

Reptile

characteristics

(glue here)

Fish

characteristics

(This page left intentionally blank)

Mammals

Cut out the hexagons and stack them with the "mammals" piece on top. Staple and add to your lapbook.

Mammals

covered in hair or fur

give birth to live young

feed milk to their babies

breathe air with lungs

(This page left intentionally blank)

Birds

Cut out the eggs and write the characteristics of birds (covered in feathers, have claws, have two wings, lay eggs).

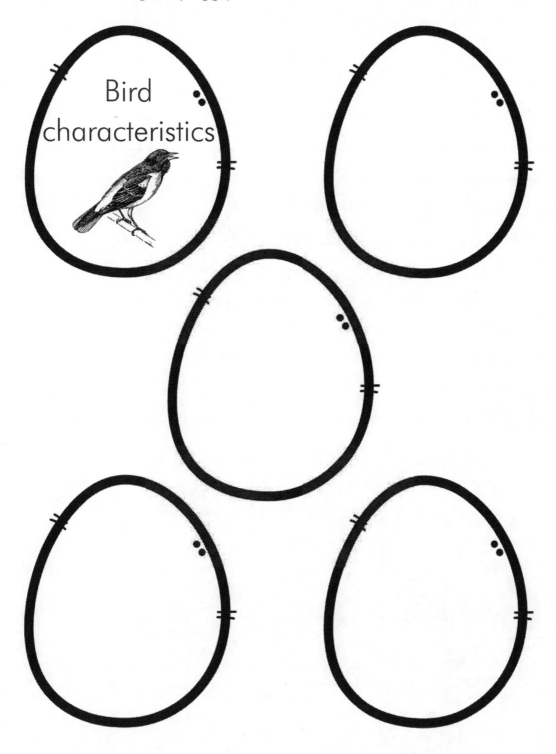

Bird characteristics

(This page left intentionally blank)

Amphibians

Cut out the lily pads. Write or glue the amphibian facts onto them.

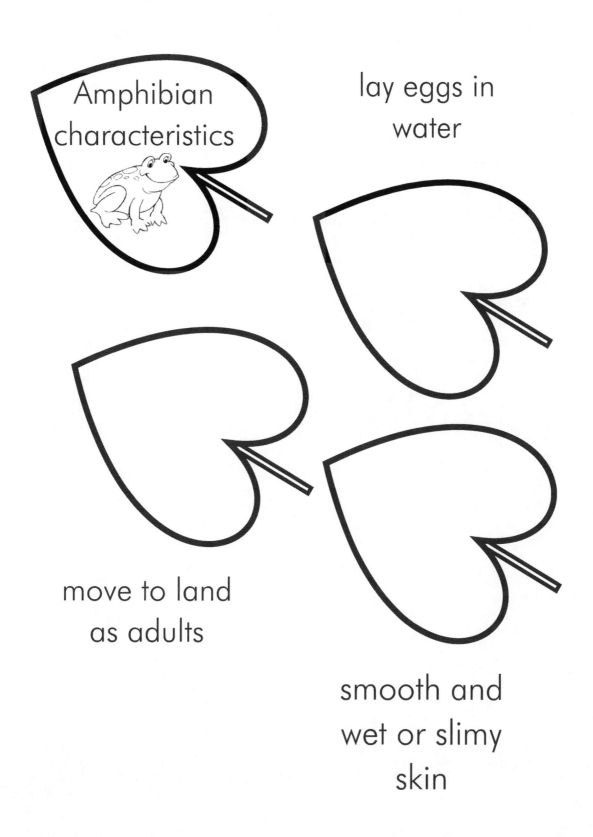

Amphibian characteristics

lay eggs in water

move to land as adults

smooth and wet or slimy skin

(This page left intentionally blank)

Echinoderms and Annelids

Cut out the rectangles and fold on the dotted line. Inside (opposite the "glue here" side), write characteristics of echinoderms (several arms or spines around a central body, usually symmetrical, hard skin) and annelids (long cylindrical body, segmented).

(glue here)

Echinoderm

characteristics

(glue here)

Annelid

characteristics

(This page left intentionally blank)

Mollusks and Arthropods

Cut out the hexagons and stack them with the "mollusks" piece on top. Staple and add to your lapbook. Do the same with the diamonds and the arthropod pieces.

Mollusk characteristics

soft body; can be covered by hard shell

in water: swim by pushing water out of their bodies

on land: move on a foot

Arthropod characteristics

hard exoskeleton and jointed limbs

Endangered Species

Cut the pages on the dotted lines and place them in this pattern: $\begin{smallmatrix}1&2\\3&4\end{smallmatrix}$ Using a single six-sided die and whatever markers you can gather (coins, different rocks, pawns from other games, etc.), take turns rolling and moving the number on the die. Follow the directions on the square you land on. Requested facts can be found throughout the board. Can you all get to the end before you go extinct?

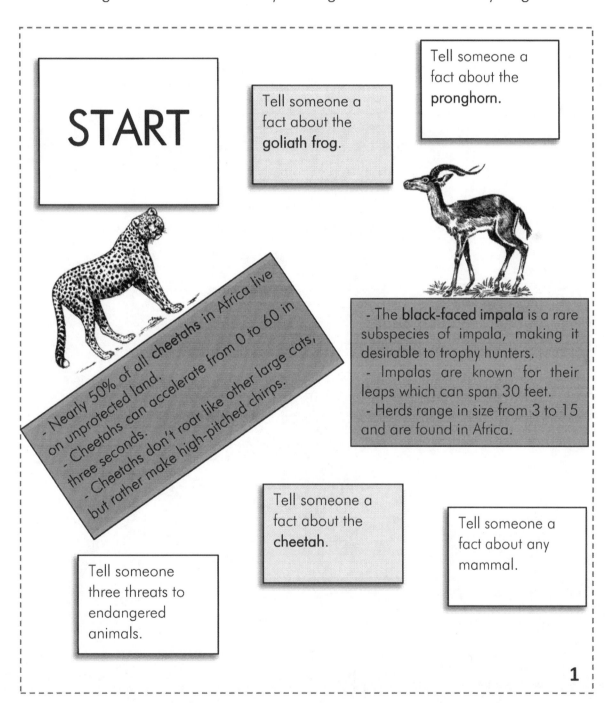

START

Tell someone a fact about the **goliath frog.**

Tell someone a fact about the **pronghorn.**

- The **black-faced impala** is a rare subspecies of impala, making it desirable to trophy hunters.
- Impalas are known for their leaps which can span 30 feet.
- Herds range in size from 3 to 15 and are found in Africa.

- Nearly 50% of all cheetahs in Africa live on unprotected land.
- Cheetahs can accelerate from 0 to 60 in three seconds.
- Cheetahs don't roar like other large cats, but rather make high-pitched chirps.

Tell someone a fact about the **cheetah.**

Tell someone a fact about any mammal.

Tell someone three threats to endangered animals.

1

(This page left intentionally blank)

Tell someone a fact about an African animal.

Tell someone a fact about the **impala**.

Your species moves from the **threatened** list to the **endangered** list. Lose a turn!

Tell someone a fact about a non-mammal.

- The **Sonoran pronghorn** is one of the most endangered animals in the United States.
- The pronghorn is the fastest land animal in North America.
- Drought is its biggest threat.

Tell someone three threats to endangered animals.

Tell someone a fact about the **blue whale**.

Tell someone a fact about the **cockatoo**.

Move forward three spaces and read that square.

Catch a poacher in the act and save an elephant. Roll again!

(This page left intentionally blank)

3

Tell someone a fact about the **goliath frog**.

Tell someone a fact about a non-mammal.

Tell someone a fact about the **impala**.

- The **blue whale** is the largest animal known to have existed.
- Whaling (hunting whales for their usable products) is its biggest threat.
- Seen regularly off the coast of California.

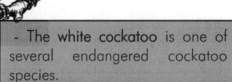

- The **white cockatoo** is one of several endangered cockatoo species.
- Its beauty makes it desirable for the pet trade
- Found in the Philippines, Indonesia, and Australia.

FINISH

Recite three things you've learned and your species will survive!

Tell any fact that hasn't been told so far to avoid extinction!

Tell someone three threats to endangered animals.

(This page left intentionally blank)

4

Tell someone a fact about the **blue whale**.

Tell someone a fact about an African animal.

Tell someone a fact about the **cockatoo**.

Discover a new population of an endangered species: roll again!

- The **goliath frog** is the largest living frog on earth.
- It is found in a few remote places such as Equatorial Guinea.
- Its biggest threat is its desirability as an exotic pet.

Tell someone a fact about the **cheetah**.

Tell someone a fact about a **mammal**.

Tell someone a fact about a non-African animal.

Make it to the finish space on your next turn or become EXTINCT.

Tell someone a fact about the **pronghorn**.

(This page left intentionally blank)

Food Web

Use the food web to answer the questions.

What are the **producers** in this food web? _____

_____

What are the **consumers** in this food web? _____

_____

What does the eagle eat? _____

_____

What eats the grass? _____

_____

What eats the mouse? _____

_____

(This page left intentionally blank)

Food Chain

Use the words above each paragraph to fill in the blanks.

food	trees	sun	energy	bottom

Plants and _____ can be found at the _____ of

the _____ chain. Unlike the foods above them, plants get _____

from the _____.

herbivores	caterpillars	plants	cattle	eaters

The _____ at the bottom of the food chain are eaten by

_____ or "plant _____." Some examples of these

would be _____ and _____.

carnivores	prey	predators	top	cheetah

At the _____ of the food chain are _____ or "meat eaters."

These animals are also known as _____ because they eat other

animals, known as their _____. An example of this animal type would be

a _____.

Zoology
Levels 1-4

(This page left intentionally blank)

The Tundra

Fill in the crossword using the clues below.

Across:

2. There is very little of this in the tundra.
5. The tundra's _____ is constantly changing.
6. The largest and most dangerous animal in the tundra. (2 words)
7. Tundra plants have adapted to low _____.
8. People worry about _____ from mines and rigs.
9. To sleep through the worst part of winter.
10. This lies six inches below the ground and remains frozen most of the year.
11. The tundra is a sensitive _____.

Down:

1. Some _____ birds live in the tundra part of the year.
3. The tundra is the _____ biome.
4. The tundra is located in this circle.
8. Permafrost can _____ plants and animals.

(This page left intentionally blank)

The Savanna

Fill in the crossword using the clues below.

Across:

2. Many animals in the savanna are plant eaters or _____.
4. During the dry season, there is a competition for this.
6. Savannas are made up of _____ and a few trees.
7. Cattle _____ limits the amount of food available for wildlife.
8. Savannas can result from _____ changes.
9. Annual _____ in the savanna is 10-30 inches.

Down:

1. The dry season in the savanna is often associated with these.
3. Many animals in the savanna are _____.
5. Elephants, zebras, and giraffes are found in _____ savannas.

(This page left intentionally blank)

The Taiga

Color this world map to show where the taiga can be found.

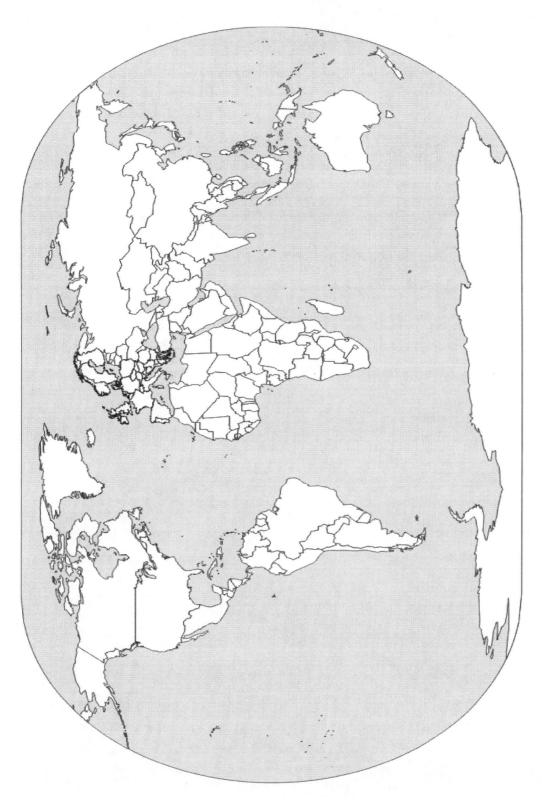

http://www.freeworldmaps.net/outline/maps/world-map-outline.gif

(This page left intentionally blank)

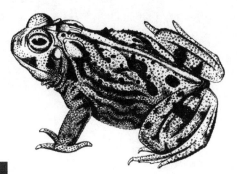

All
About
Frogs

(This page left intentionally blank)

Frog Facts

Cut out each book as one piece: two rectangles and a frog on a lily pad. Fold like a tent on the solid line so that the question is on the front. Answer the question on the inside (opposite "glue here") and then fold the frog up to hold the book closed. The answers to the questions are also included if you prefer to cut them out and paste them in each book. If you're assembling as a lapbook, glue to your file folder or poster board on the "glue here" side.

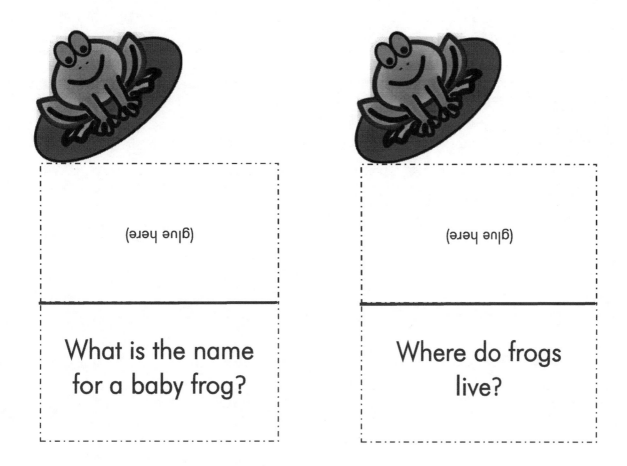

(glue here)

What is the name for a baby frog?

(glue here)

Where do frogs live?

A baby frog is called a tadpole or pollywog.

Frogs live in ponds, swamps, woodlands, ditches, and marshes.

(This page left intentionally blank)

Frog Facts

(glue here)

What do frogs eat?

(glue here)

Where do frogs lay their eggs?

Frogs eat worms, small insects, and spiders.

Frogs lay their eggs in water.

(This page left intentionally blank)

Frog Facts

(glue here)

What is a frog's
skin like?

(glue here)

What do frogs do in
winter?

A frog's skin is smooth
and wet.

Frogs hibernate in the
winter.

(This page left intentionally blank)

Frog Facts

(glue here)

_____

When do frogs hunt?

(glue here)

_____

How do frogs catch their prey?

Frogs hunt at night.

Frogs have long, sticky tongues that they use to catch their prey.

(This page left intentionally blank)

Parts of a Frog

Cut out the book as one piece and fold it in half. Glue the separate frog onto the inside of the book (opposite "glue here"). Label these parts of the frog: eye, ear drum, nostril, vocal sac, hind leg, and webbed foot. If you're making a lapbook, glue the "glue here" side down.

(glue here)

Parts of a Frog

(This page left intentionally blank)

(This page left intentionally blank)

Cut out the rectangle as one piece. Fold the left side in (on the line at **A**), and fold the right side in (on the line at **B**). Cut on the dotted lines so that each frog part is a strip you can open to the fold. On the inside (opposite "glue here"), write about each frog part. If you're making a lapbook, glue the "glue here" side down.

Frog feet

Frog teeth

Frog skin

Frog ears

A →

(glue here)

B ↓

Frog
Anatomy

(This page left intentionally blank)

Tadpole or Frog

Cut out the book as one piece and fold it in half. On the inside, write or glue Tadpole at the top of one page and Frog at the top of the other. Write or glue the individual facts on the correct pages. If you're making a lapbook, glue the "glue here" side down.

(glue here)

Tadpole
or
Frog

Tadpole

has tail growing to legs

eaten by water bugs

breathes with gills

lives in water

senses: smell and vibration

Frog

has four legs

eaten by snakes and birds

breathes with lungs through skin

lives near water on land

senses: sight and hearing

(This page left intentionally blank)

Frog or Toad

Fill in the Venn diagram with frog and toad facts. Add to your lapbook if you're making one.

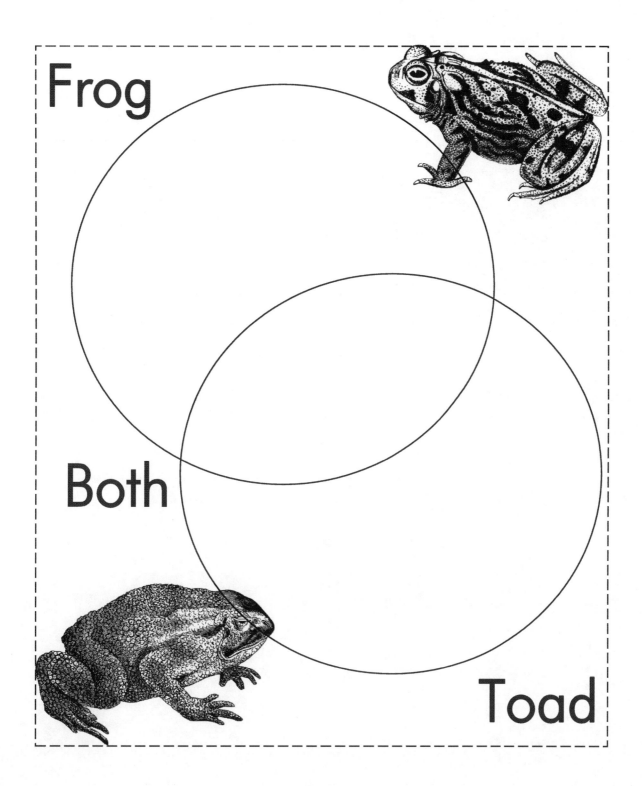

Frog

Both

Toad

(This page left intentionally blank)

Frog Facts

Use the hexagons to record other frog facts. You can staple the hexagons together and glue the back one to your lapbook if you're making one.

Other Frog Facts

(This page left intentionally blank)

Hibernation

Migration

Adaptation

(This page left intentionally blank)

Wake or Sleep

Cut out the rectangle as one piece and fold on the center line. Cut on the dotted line to the center fold. Inside (opposite the "glue here" side), glue each animal under the appropriate flap based on whether it wakes to eat or sleeps all winter.

(glue here)

Wakes to eat

Sleeps all winter

brown bat	ladybug	gopher	turtle	squirrel
chipmunk	snake	frog	bear	skunk

(This page left intentionally blank)

Zoology
Levels 1-4

Hibernation

Cut out each piece as one and fold them in half. Answer the question about hibernation inside that piece. In the squirrel piece, write how animals prepare for winter by continuously eating.

(glue here)

What is hibernation?

(This page left intentionally blank)

Hibernation

Cut out the rectangle as one piece. Fold the left side in (on the line at A), and fold the right side in (on the line at B). Cut on the dotted line so that there are two strips you can open to the fold. On the inside (opposite "glue here"), write about the changes in breathing and body temperature an animal in hibernation experiences.

Breathing

Body Temperature

A →

(glue here)

B ↓

What bodily changes occur during hibernation?

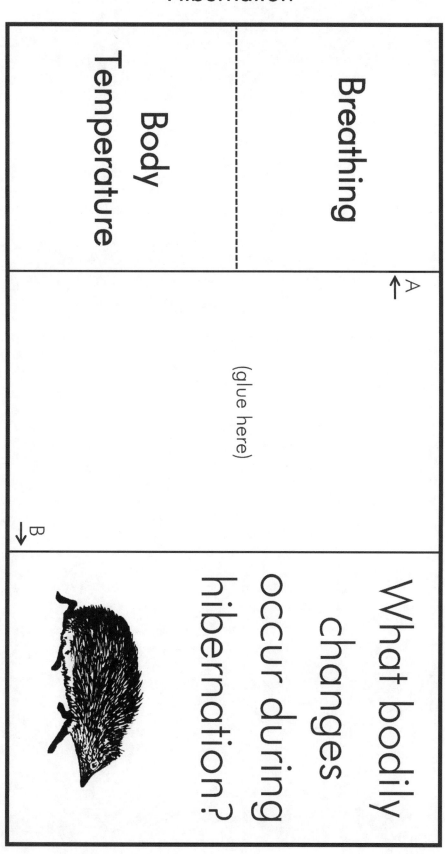

Zoology
Levels 1-4

(This page left intentionally blank)

Turtles and Snakes

Cut out the rectangle as one piece and fold on the center line. Cut on the dotted line. Write the answer inside on the backside of the flaps. On the inside (opposite the "glue here" side), write WHY turtles and snakes sleep for the winter where they do. Use complete sentences.

(glue here)

Where do they sleep?

Turtles

Snakes

(This page left intentionally blank)

Migration

Cut out the rectangles and fold on the dotted line. Inside (opposite the "glue here" side), answer the questions in complete sentences.

(glue here)

What is migration?

(glue here)

Why do some birds fly south for the winter?

(This page left intentionally blank)

Migration

Cut out the rectangle as one piece and fold on the center line. On the inside (opposite the "glue here" side), answer the question. On the next page, draw the migration routes for the birds listed. Be sure to color in the key with the colors you use for each bird's route.

(glue here)

Which birds fly south for the winter?

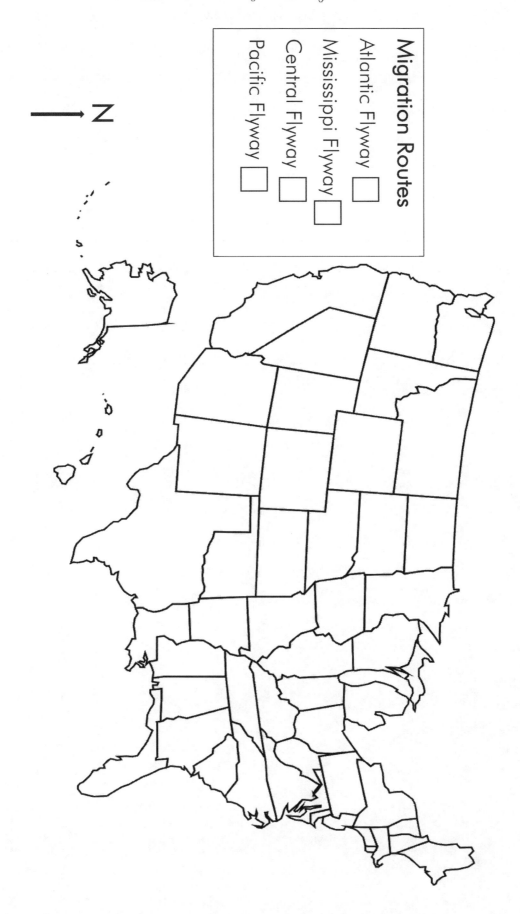

Migration Routes

Atlantic Flyway ☐

Mississippi Flyway ☐

Central Flyway ☐

Pacific Flyway ☐

N →

(This page left intentionally blank)

Adaptation

Cut out the hexagons and fold on the middle line. Inside (opposite the "glue here" side), answer the questions in complete sentences.

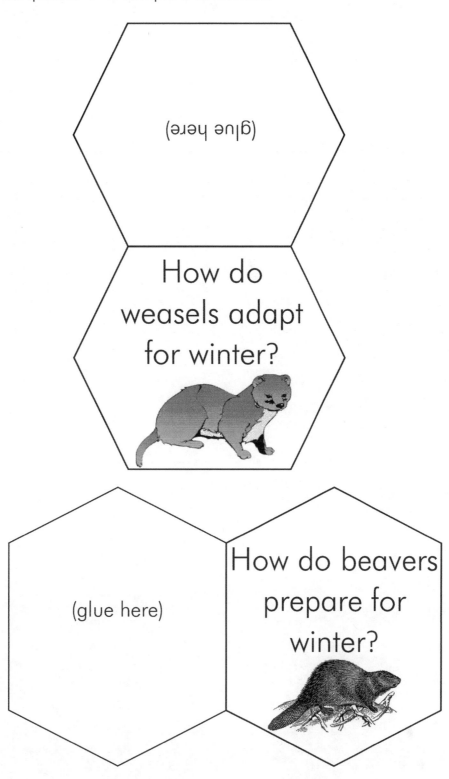

(glue here)

How do weasels adapt for winter?

(glue here)

How do beavers prepare for winter?

(This page left intentionally blank)

Adaptation

Cut out the hexagons and fold on the middle line. Inside (opposite the "glue here" side), answer the questions in complete sentences.

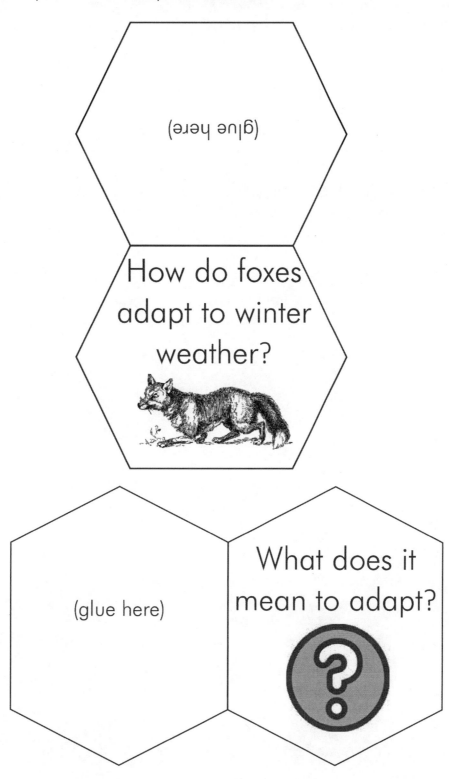

(glue here)

How do foxes adapt to winter weather?

(glue here)

What does it mean to adapt?

(This page left intentionally blank)

All
About
Lizards

Zoology
Levels 1-4

(This page left intentionally blank)

Classification

Cut out the rectangle as one piece. Fold the left side in (on the line at **A**), and fold the right side in (on the line at **B**). Cut on the dotted lines so that Kingdom, Phylum, Class, and Order are strips you can open to the fold. On the inside (opposite "glue here"), fill in the information.

Kingdom

Phylum

Class

Order

A →

(glue here)

B →

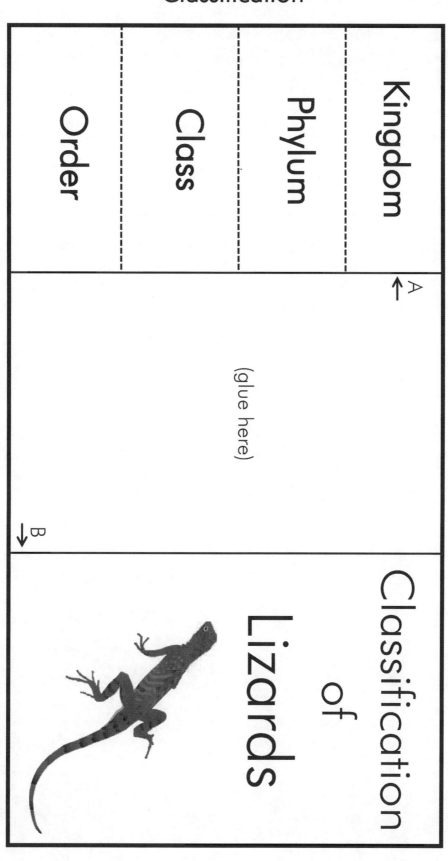

Classification
of
Lizards

(This page left intentionally blank)

Reptiles

Cut out the hexagons and fold on the middle line. Inside (opposite the "glue here" side), write the characteristics of reptiles and some examples of other reptiles.

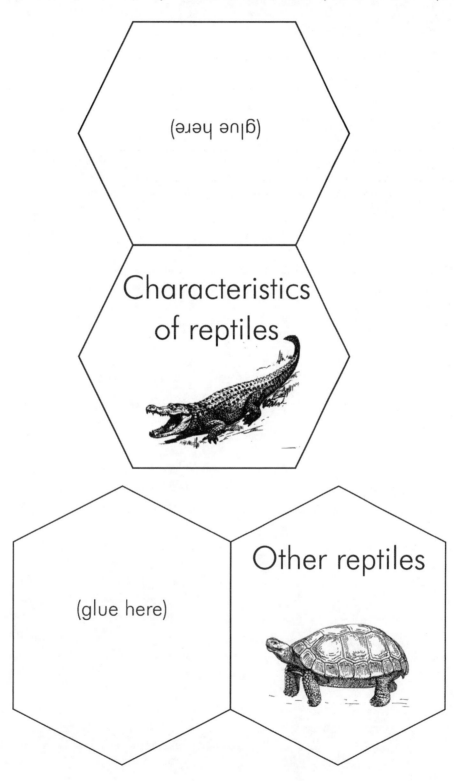

(glue here)

Characteristics of reptiles

(glue here)

Other reptiles

(This page left intentionally blank)

Vocabulary

Cut out the rocks and write the definitions to the vocabulary words they contain.
Use the lizard as the cover piece and staple on the side.

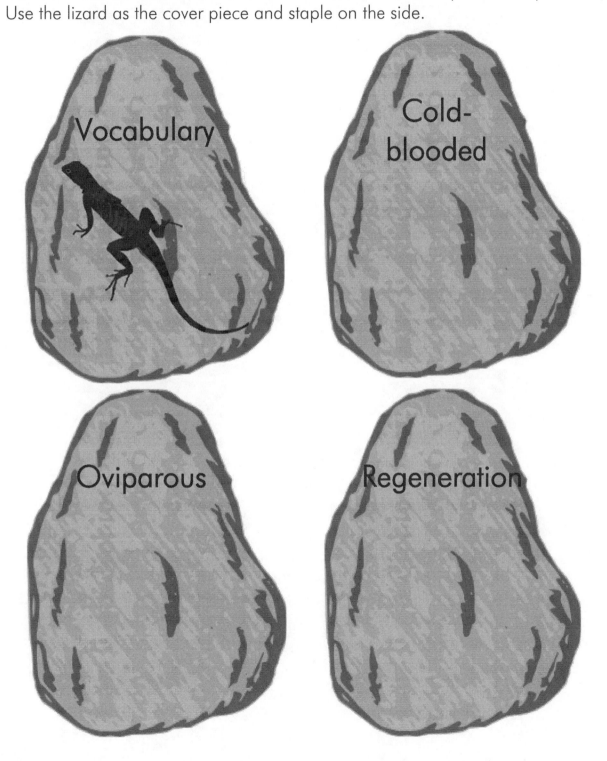

Vocabulary

Cold-blooded

Oviparous

Regeneration

(This page left intentionally blank)

Location

Color in the locations on the world map where lizards are found. You can make a key and color different colors for different types of lizards if you want to do further research. Cut the big rectangle as one piece and fold the outside squares to cover the world map. Glue the label pieces on top of the folded piece.

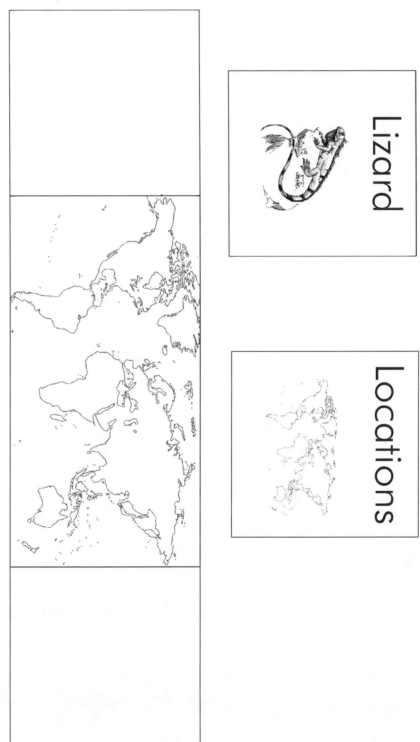

(This page left intentionally blank)

Predators

Cut out the rectangle as one piece and fold on the dotted line. Inside (opposite the "glue here" side), write some of the predators of lizards. You can also draw pictures if you'd like.

(glue here)

- -

Predators of lizards

(This page left intentionally blank)

Defense

Cut out the rectangle as one piece and fold on the dotted line. Inside (opposite the "glue here" side), write or cut and paste the different types of defense mechanisms a lizard has.

(glue here)

- -

A lizard's
defense

camouflage	sharp spines	slippery scales

strong, swinging tails

(This page left intentionally blank)

Lizard senses

Cut each piece out in full (don't cut off the tab label). Write information on each piece. Stack the pieces in this order top to bottom: Lizard senses, sight, smell, hearing.

Lizard senses

How do lizards see?

sight

(This page left intentionally blank)

How do lizards smell?

smell

How do lizards hear?

hearing

(This page left intentionally blank)

Lizard Food

Cut out the rectangle and fold on the dotted line. Inside (opposite the "glue here" side), write what lizards eat. You can draw pictures if you'd like.

(glue here)

What do lizards eat?

(This page left intentionally blank)

Types of Lizards

Cut each piece out in full and fold each piece on the dotted line. Write facts about each type of lizard inside the piece, then glue the three small pieces side by side inside of the large piece.

(glue here)

Types of Lizards

(This page left intentionally blank)

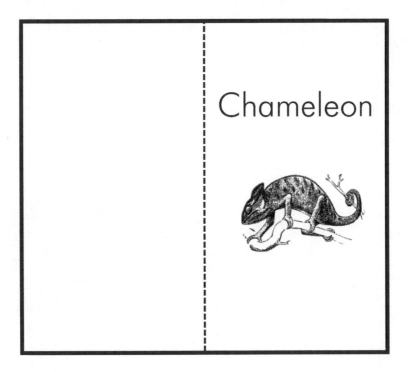

Chameleon

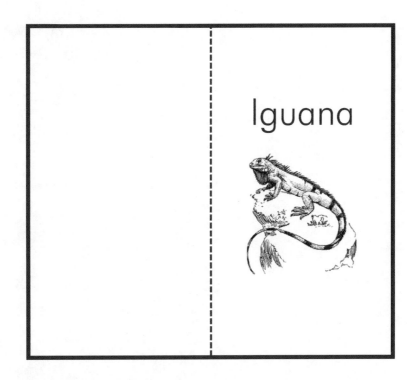

Iguana

(This page left intentionally blank)

Gila
monster

(This page left intentionally blank)

Lizard facts

Cut out the hexagons and stack them with the "facts" piece on top. Fill in the blank pieces with any facts you've learned about lizards that you didn't get to include elsewhere in the book. Staple and add to your lapbook.

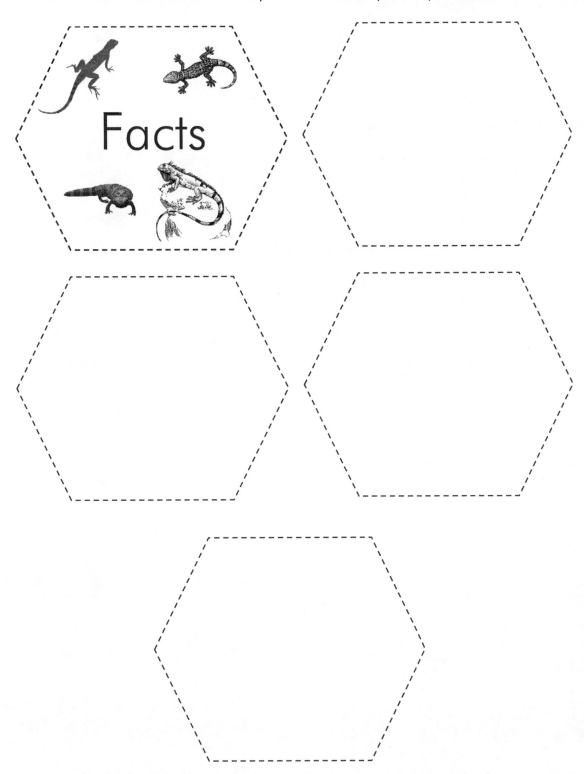

(This page left intentionally blank)

All
About
Dinosaurs

(This page left intentionally blank)

Dinosaurs

Cut out the rectangles and fold on the dotted line. Inside (opposite the "glue here" side), define dinosaur on the dinosaur piece, and tell what a paleontologist does on the paleontologist piece.

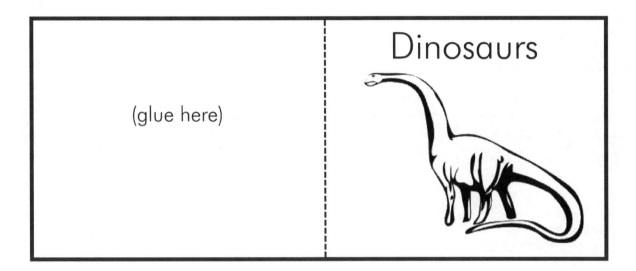

(glue here)

Dinosaurs

(glue here)

Paleontologist

(This page left intentionally blank)

Dinosaurs

Cut out each piece as one (do not cut off the tabs). Cut and glue each dinosaur to the continent where it has been discovered. Assemble as a tabbed book – the cover goes on top, then North America, South America, Africa, Europe, Asia, Australia, Antarctica.

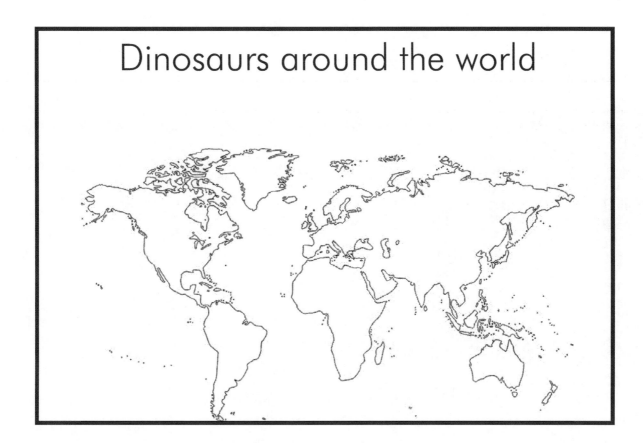

Dinosaurs around the world

(This page left intentionally blank)

Zoology
Levels 1-4

Lesson
53

North
America

Triceratops

(This page left intentionally blank)

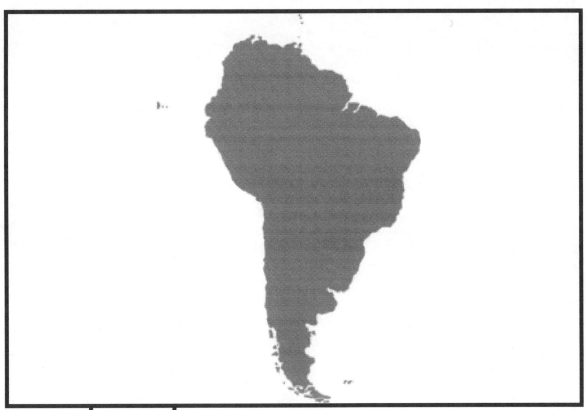

South
America

Iguanodon

(This page left intentionally blank)

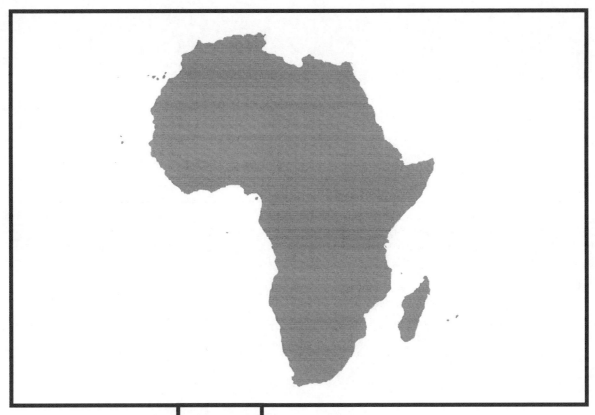

Africa

Brachiosaurus

(This page left intentionally blank)

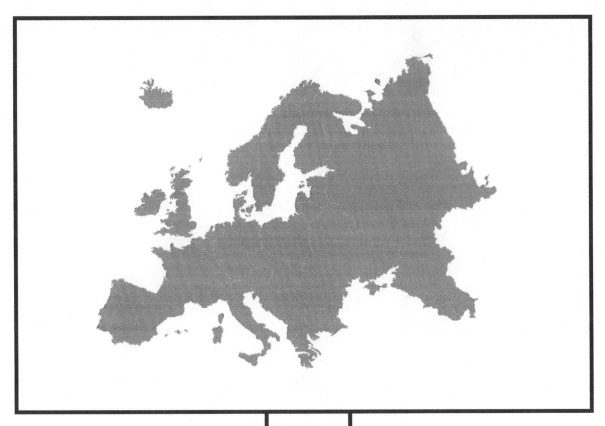

Europe

Apatosaurus   Stegosaurus

Zoology
Levels 1-4

(This page left intentionally blank)

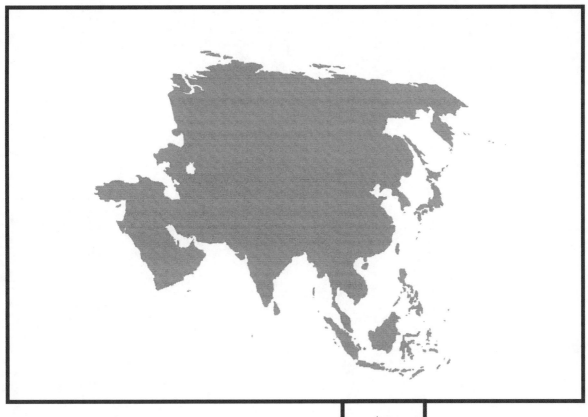

Asia

Velociraptor

Tyrannosaurus

Zoology
Levels 1-4

(This page left intentionally blank)

Australia

Allosaurus

(This page left intentionally blank)

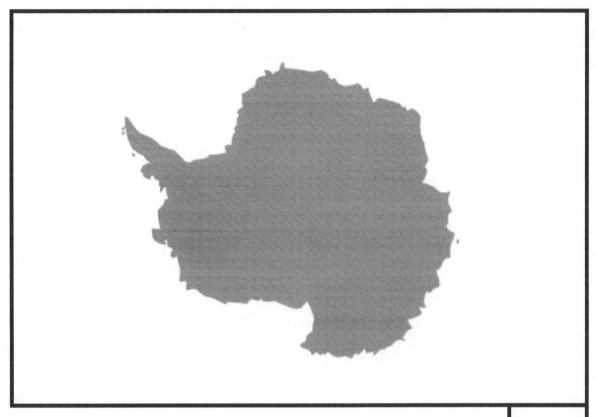

Antarctica

Ankylosaurus

(This page left intentionally blank)

Dinosaurs

Color the graph up to the right number for each dinosaur.

	Tyrannosaurus	Iguanadon	Triceratops	Utahraptor	Stegosaurus	Velociraptor
40 feet						
38 feet						
36 feet						
34 feet						
32 feet						
30 feet						
28 feet						
26 feet						
24 feet						
22 feet						
20 feet						
18 feet						
16 feet						
14 feet						
12 feet						
10 feet						
8 feet						
6 feet						
4 feet						
2 feet						

Dinosaur Height Graph

(This page left intentionally blank)

Dinosaur Diets

Cut out the rectangle as one piece and fold on the center line. Cut on the dotted line to the center fold. Inside (opposite the "glue here" side), write what the dinosaurs ate before and after the fall.

(glue here)

Before the Fall

After the Fall

(This page left intentionally blank)

What Happened After the Flood

Cut around the outside of the first circle, as well as along the dotted lines to cut out the "cut out here" section. Cut around the outside of the second circle. Stack the first circle on the second circle and secure with a brad.

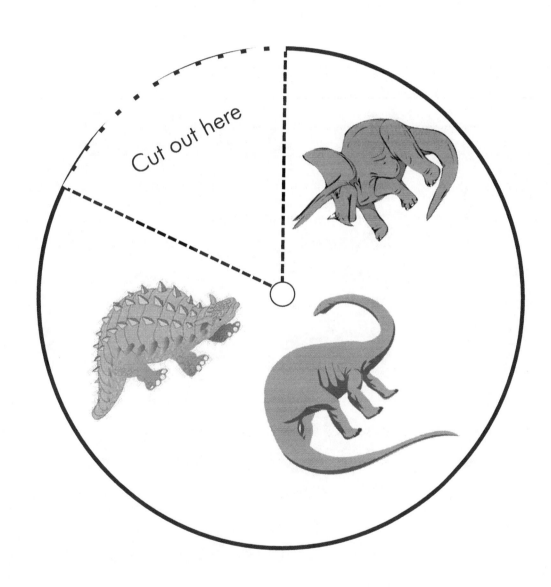

Cut out here

Zoology
Levels 1-4

(This page left intentionally blank)

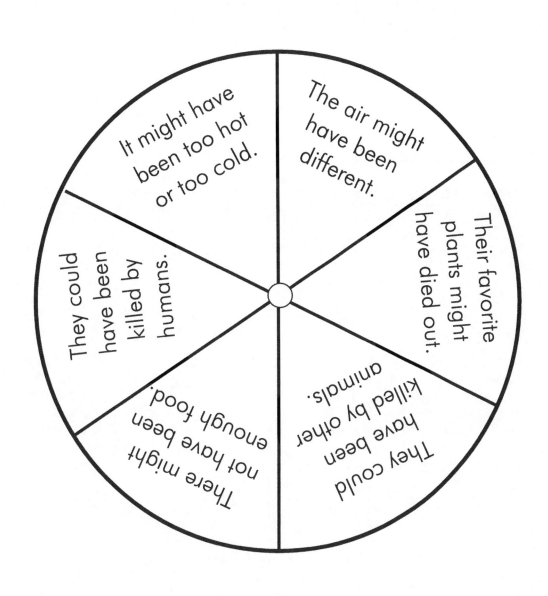

(This page left intentionally blank)

Bible Verses

Cut out as one piece. Fold up bottom. Then fold back side tabs and secure to the back flap. You have made a pocket to hold the verse cards in your lapbook. Cut out the verse cards. Once you read through them, store them in the pocket.

Dinosaurs

and the

Bible

(This page left intentionally blank)

Genesis 1:21

"God created the great sea monsters and every living creature that moves, with which the waters swarmed after their kind, and every winged bird after its kind; and God saw that it was good."

Job 41:1, 9

"Can you draw out Leviathan with a fishhook? Or press down his tongue with a cord?"

"Any hope of subduing him is false; the mere sight of him is overpowering."

Job 40:15-18

"Behold now, Behemoth, which I made as well as you; He eats grass like an ox. Behold now, his strength in his loins and his power in the muscles of his belly. He bends his tail like a cedar; the sinews of his thighs are knit together. His bones are tubes of bronze; his limbs are like bars of iron."

(This page left intentionally blank)

Lesson 56+

Lapbook pieces

(glue here)

A

B

Cut out the rectangle as one piece. Fold the left side in (on the line at **A**), and fold the right side in (on the line at **B**). Cut on the dotted lines so you have four strips you can label and open to the fold. On the inside (opposite "glue here"), write your information. On the right panel, create a title and add artwork if you'd like.

(This page left intentionally blank)

Lapbook pieces

Cut out the rectangle as one piece and fold on the center line. Cut on the dotted line to the center fold. Label the two flaps. Inside (opposite the "glue here" side), write your information.

(glue here)

(This page left intentionally blank)

Lapbook pieces

Cut out the rectangles and fold on the dotted line. Label the right side and add artwork if you'd like. Inside (opposite the "glue here" side), write your information.

(glue here)

(glue here)

(This page left intentionally blank)

(glue here)

(glue here)

(This page left intentionally blank)

Lesson
56+

Lapbook Pieces

Cut out the hexagons. Add a title and/or artwork to one piece and information to the other pieces. Stack them and staple on the side to make a book.

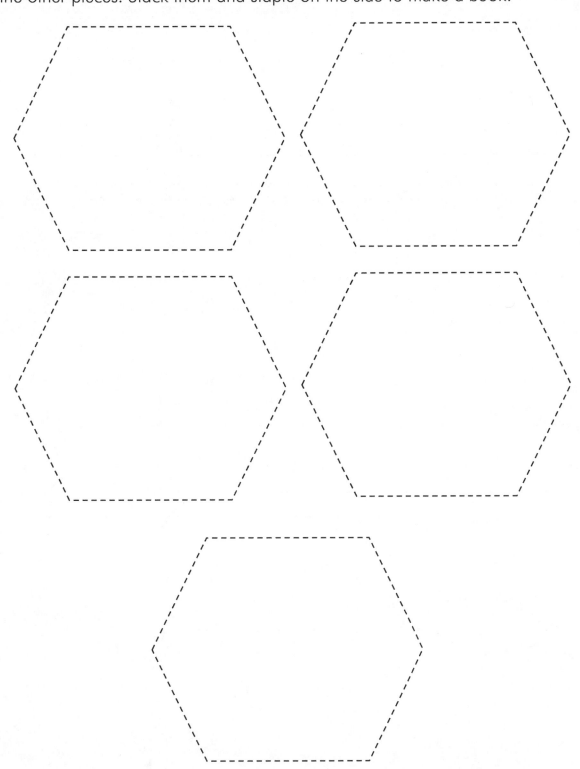

(This page left intentionally blank)

Lapbook pieces

Cut out the rectangle as one piece and fold on the dotted line. Give the piece a title and/or artwork. Inside (opposite the "glue here" side), write your information.

(glue here)

(This page left intentionally blank)

(glue here)

(This page left intentionally blank)

Lapbook pieces

Cut each piece out in full (don't cut off the tab label). The piece without the tab is the cover – add a title and/or artwork. Be sure to label each tab and stack them in order: cover, left tab, center tab, right tab.

(This page left intentionally blank)

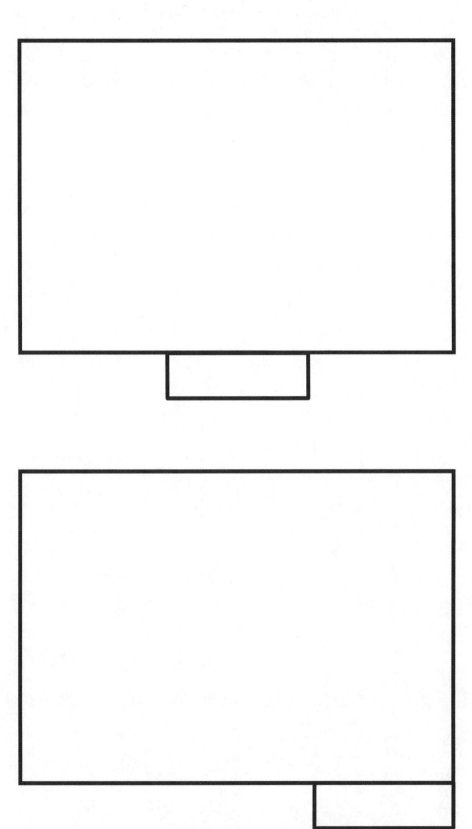

(This page left intentionally blank)

Lapbook Pieces

Cut each piece out in full and fold each piece on the dotted line. Write a title on the big book. Give each small book a topic and put facts inside. Glue the three small pieces side by side inside of the large piece.

(glue here)

(This page left intentionally blank)

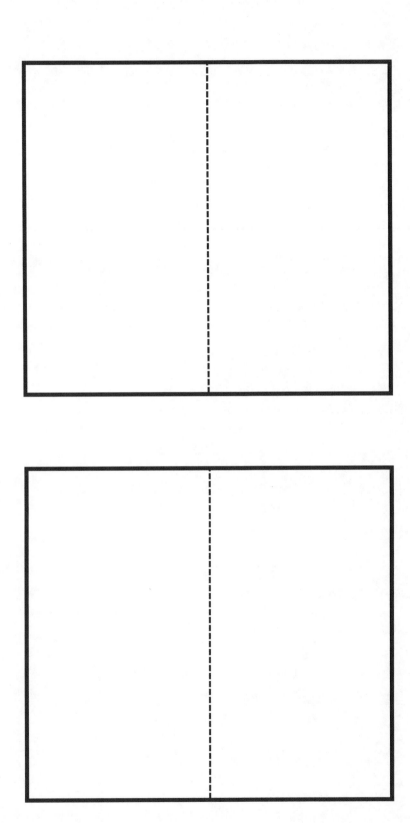

(This page left intentionally blank)

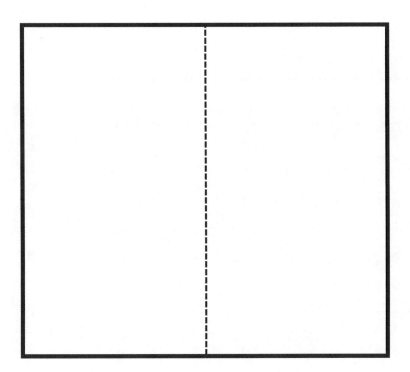

(This page left intentionally blank)

Lapbook pieces

Cut around the outside of the first circle, as well as along the dotted lines to cut out the "cut out here" section. Put a title and/or artwork on this circle. Cut around the outside of the second circle. Fill each wedge of the circle with a fact (you can add more artwork if you have too many wedges). Stack the first circle on the second circle and secure with a brad.

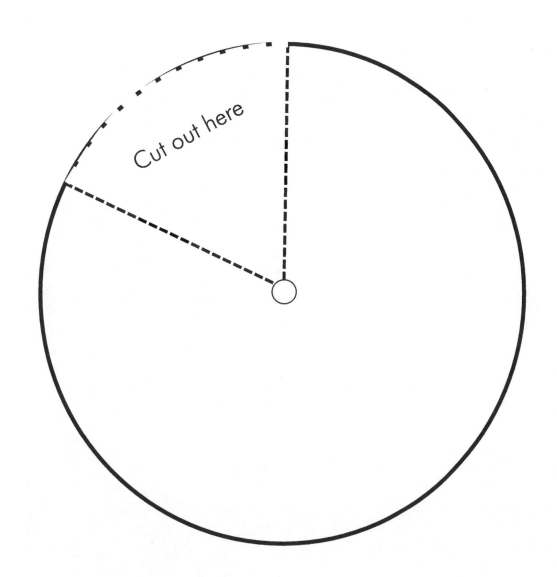

(This page left intentionally blank)

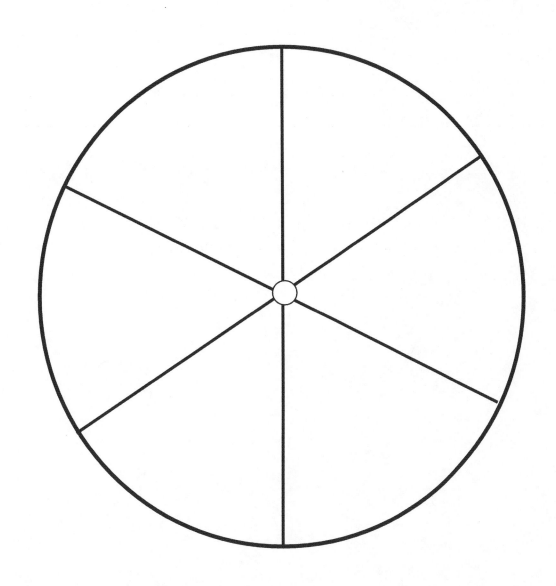

(This page left intentionally blank)

Bird Parts

Label the parts of the bird using the words in the box.

beak	breast	claws
crown	tail feathers	wing feathers

(This page left intentionally blank)

Bird Adaptations

Compare and contrast birds using the Venn diagrams below.

Beaks

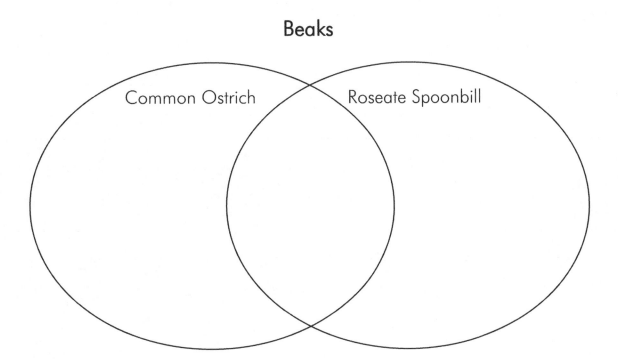

Common Ostrich

Roseate Spoonbill

Movement

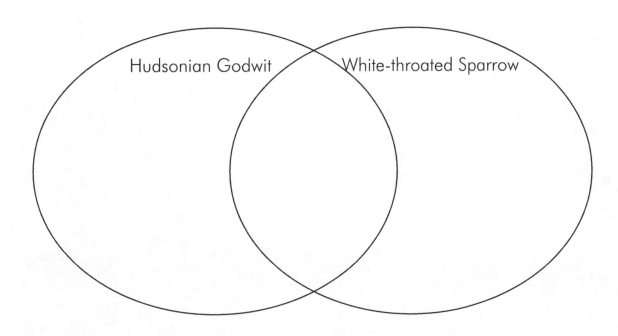

Hudsonian Godwit

White-throated Sparrow

(This page left intentionally blank)

Bird Songs

Match the bird with the sound of its song or call.

Crow

wha-cheer, wha-cheer

Mourning Dove

hoo-oo, hoo-hoo-hoo

Northern Cardinal

chicka-dee-dee-dee

Blue Jay

caw, caw

Black-capped Chickadee

jay, jay

(This page left intentionally blank)

Beaks

Match the beak to the tool it most resembles.

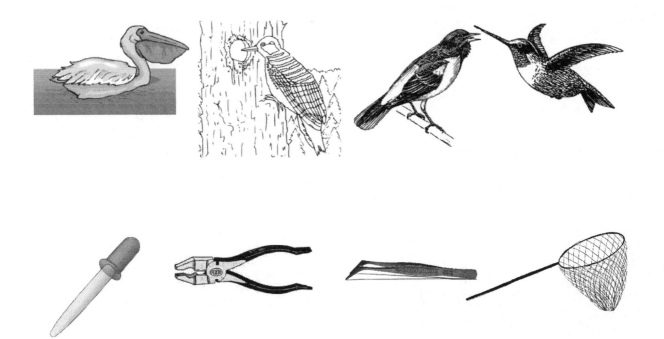

Match the bird to the food they eat. The tools their beaks resemble can be a clue to the food they eat.

(This page left intentionally blank)

Beaks

Choose some small items to simulate bird-sized food. Beads, rubber bugs, leaves, or any other small items you can find will work well. Fill in the top boxes of the table with the types of "food" you are using. Then keep track of how many of each item you're able to pick up with your "beak."

Type of food → Type of beak ↓			
chopsticks			
toothpick			
tongs			
clothespin			

(This page left intentionally blank)

Wing Shape

Match the wing shape with the type of flight.

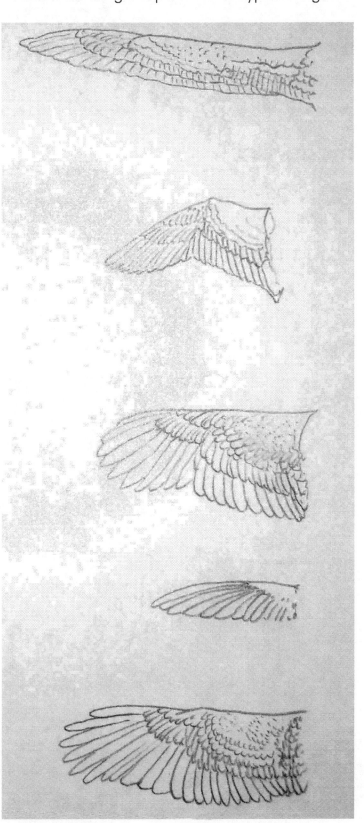

soaring up high

rapid take offs
and easy turns

gliding over
water

hovering

high speed

(This page left intentionally blank)

Flapping Experiment

Record the number of flaps you do in each 30-second trial.

Wing type	Elbows In	Arms Out	With Weights
Number of flaps			

Graph your results!

Number of flaps		Elbows In	Arms Out	With Weights
	40			
	38			
	36			
	34			
	32			
	30			
	28			
	26			
	24			
	22			
	20			
	18			
	16			
	14			
	12			
	10			
	8			
	6			
	4			
	2			
	0	Elbows In	Arms Out	With Weights

(This page left intentionally blank)

All
About
Eagles

(This page left intentionally blank)

Eagle stats

Size

Weight

Wingspan

Speed

A →

(glue here)

B →

Bald Eagle Stats

Cut out the rectangle as one piece. Fold the left side in (on the line at **A**), and fold the right side in (on the line at **B**). Cut on the dotted lines so that the four categories are strips you can open to the fold. On the inside (opposite "glue here"), write the information for that category.

(This page left intentionally blank)

Where Do They Live?

Cut out the rectangles and fold on the dotted line. Inside (opposite the "glue here" side), write about bald eagle habitats and nests.

(glue here) | Habitat

(glue here) | Nests

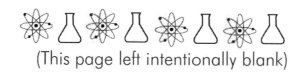

(This page left intentionally blank)

Eagle Diet

Cut around the outside of the first circle, as well as along the dotted lines to cut out the "cut out here" section. Cut around the outside of the second circle. Stack the first circle on the second circle and secure with a brad.

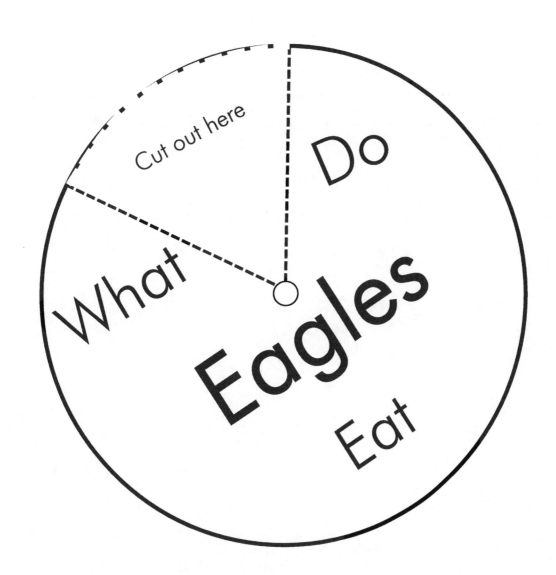

Cut out here

Do

What

Eagles

Eat

(This page left intentionally blank)

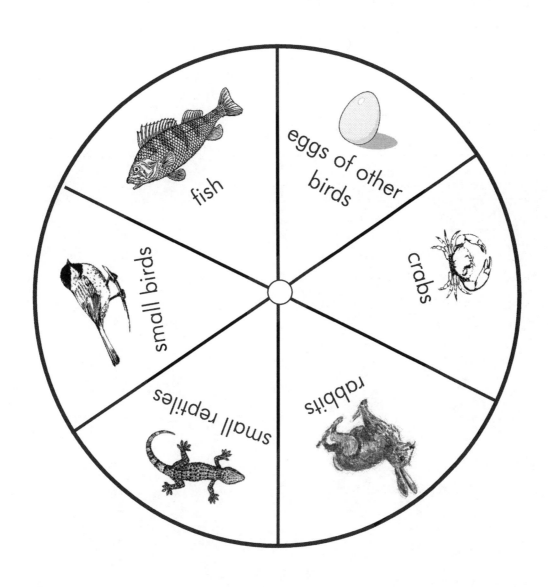

(This page left intentionally blank)

Eagles in the Nations

Cut out the rectangle as one piece and fold on the dotted line. Inside (opposite the "glue here" side), write or paste the various countries around the world that use the eagle as the national bird.

(glue here)

National Bird

Zoology
Levels 1-4

(This page left intentionally blank)

Germany

Kazakhstan

Mexico

United States

Austria

(This page left intentionally blank)

Bible Verses

Cut out as one piece. Fold up bottom. Then fold back side tabs and secure to the back flap. You have made a pocket to hold the verse cards in your lapbook. Cut out the verse cards. Use the blank cards to copy down more verses if you'd like – there are lots of mentions of eagles in the Bible! Store them in the pocket.

Eagles
in the
Bible

(This page left intentionally blank)

Psalm 103:5

"He fills my life with good things. My youth is renewed like the eagle's."

Exodus 19:4

"You have seen what I did to the Egyptians. You know how I carried you on eagles' wings and brought you to myself."

Isaiah 40:31

"But those who trust in the Lord will find new strength. They will soar high on wings like eagles. They will run and not grow weary. They will walk and not faint."

(This page left intentionally blank)

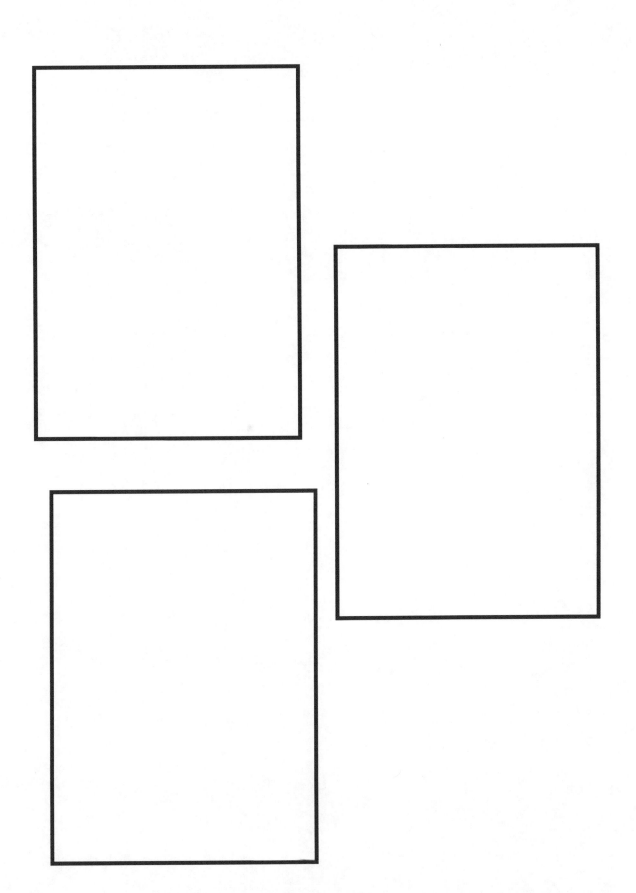

(This page left intentionally blank)

Location

Color in the locations on the world map where eagles are found. You can make a key and color different colors for different times of the year if you want to do further research. Cut the big rectangle as one piece and fold the outside squares to cover the world map. Glue the label pieces on top of the folded piece.

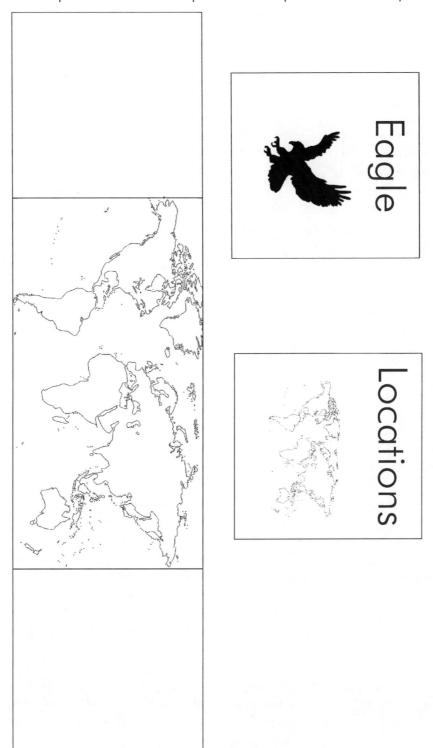

Eagle

Locations

(This page left intentionally blank)

Other Facts

Cut out the eggs and write other interesting facts you've learned about bald eagles.

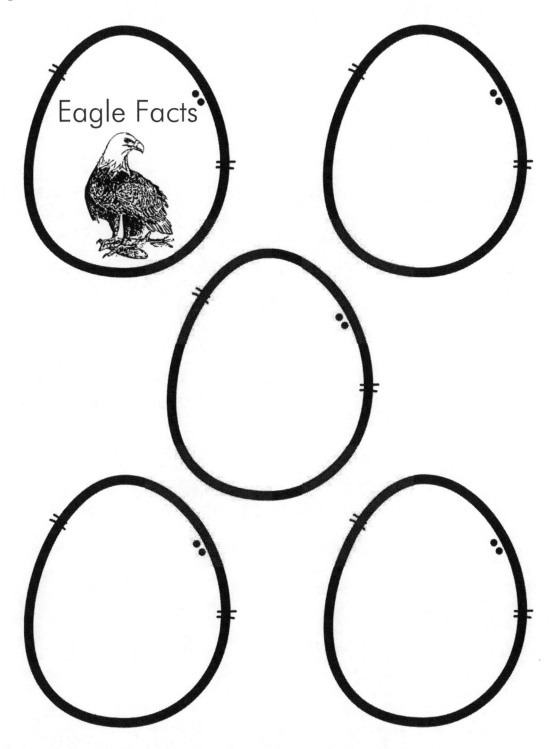

Eagle Facts

(This page left intentionally blank)

All
About
Bees

(This page left intentionally blank)

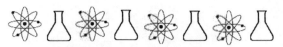

Types of Bees

Cut each piece out in full (don't cut off the tab label). Write information on each piece. Stack the pieces in this order top to bottom: types of bees, drone, worker, queen.

drone

(This page left intentionally blank)

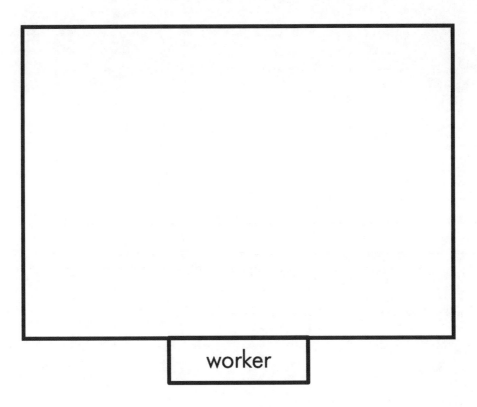

worker

queen

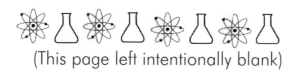

(This page left intentionally blank)

Worker Bees

Cut out the rectangle as one piece and fold on the dotted line. Inside (opposite the "glue here" side), write or glue the various jobs of a worker bee.

(glue here)

Worker Bees

collect nectar and pollen   make honey   clean

build the comb   tend to the queen   feed babies

maintain hive temperature   guard the hive

(This page left intentionally blank)

Bee Bodies

Use the directions on the site to label the bee body.

(This page left intentionally blank)

Bee Facts

Cut the honeycombs and stack them. Read the bee facts. Which one is your favorite? Tell someone else!

One bee colony can eat up to 200 pounds of honey a year!

One pound of honey = 2 million flowers, 25,000 trips to and from the hive, 55,000 miles of travel.

One bee can visit more than 2,000 flowers a day.

Queen bees can lay up to 2,000 eggs in a day.

(This page left intentionally blank)

Bee Hive

Trace, color, and cut out the hexagons. Glue them together on another piece of paper, all touching like a honeycomb.

(This page left intentionally blank)

Honey Heisters

Cut out the rectangle as one piece and fold on the center line. Inside (opposite the "glue here" side), glue (or write) the honey lovers that pose a threat to a bee's hive.

(glue here)

Honey Heisters

bears

humans

skunks

wasps

bees from
other hives

(This page left intentionally blank)

Bee Communication

Cut around the outside of the first circle, as well as along the dotted lines to cut out the "cut out here" section. Cut around the outside of the second circle. Stack the first circle on the second circle and secure with a brad.

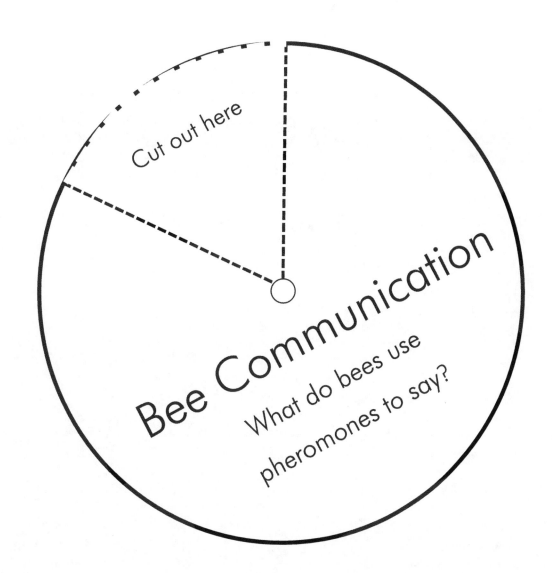

Cut out here

Bee Communication

What do bees use pheromones to say?

(This page left intentionally blank)

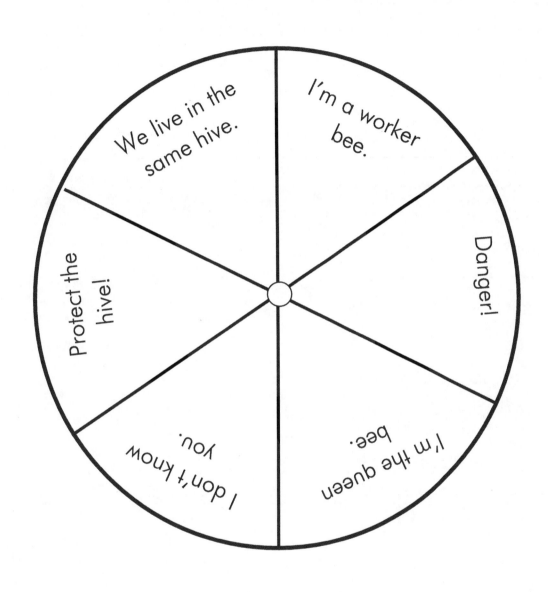

(This page left intentionally blank)

Bee dances

Cut out the rectangle as one piece. Fold the left side in (on the line at **A**), and fold the right side in (on the line at **B**). Cut on the dotted lines so that the 5 sections are strips you can open to the fold. On the inside (opposite "glue here"), write or paste what each bee dance means.

Round dance	Waggle dance	Waggle dance up	Waggle dance right	Waggle dance left

↑ A

(glue here)

↓ B

Bee Dances

(This page left intentionally blank)

Round dance:

Tells bees a food
source is near the hive

Waggle dance:

Tells bees a food source
is far from the hive

Tells workers to fly
toward the sun

Tells workers to fly to
the left of the sun

Tells workers to fly to
the right of the sun

(This page left intentionally blank)

Honey

Put the honey facts into the honey jar.

Bees suck nectar out of flowers
using their proboscises

They return to the hive and pass
the nectar to other bees

(This page left intentionally blank)

House bees chew the nectar for about 30 minutes

Worker bees spread the nectar all over the honeycomb to dry

Bees fan the nectar with their wings to help it dry faster

When honey is ready, the bees plug the honeycomb with wax

(This page left intentionally blank)

Pollination

Cut out the rectangles and fold on the dotted line. Inside (opposite the "glue here" side), write about how bees use pollen to make food and how they also help flowers by carrying pollen from one flower to another, which enables them to make seeds and fruit.

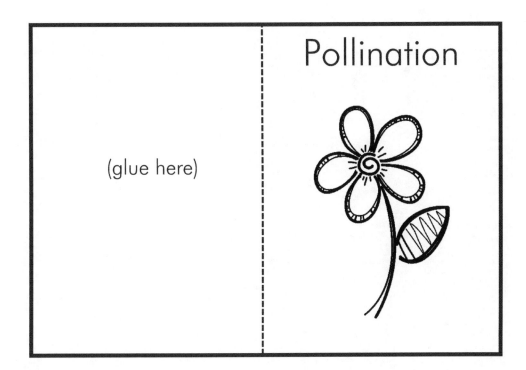

(This page left intentionally blank)

Royal Jelly

Cut out the rectangle as one piece and fold on the center line. Cut on the dotted line to the center fold. Inside (opposite the "glue here" side), write the answers to the questions.

(glue here)

What is royal jelly?

Who eats it?

(This page left intentionally blank)

Bee Life Cycle

Cut around the outside of the first circle, as well as along the dotted lines to cut out the "cut out here" section. Cut around the outside of the second circle. Stack the first circle on the second circle and secure with a brad.

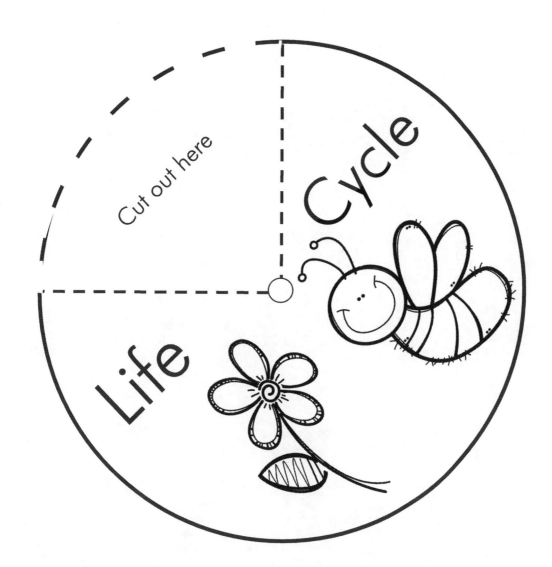

(This page left intentionally blank)

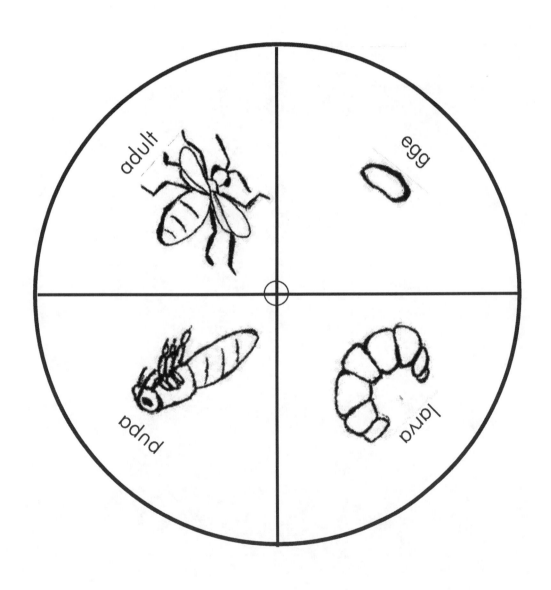

(This page left intentionally blank)

All
About
Worms

(This page left intentionally blank)

Earthworm Vocabulary

Cut out as one piece. Fold up bottom. Then fold back side tabs and secure to the back flap. You have made a pocket to hold the vocabulary cards in your lapbook. Cut out the vocabulary cards and glue the definition onto the word card. Store the word cards in the pocket.

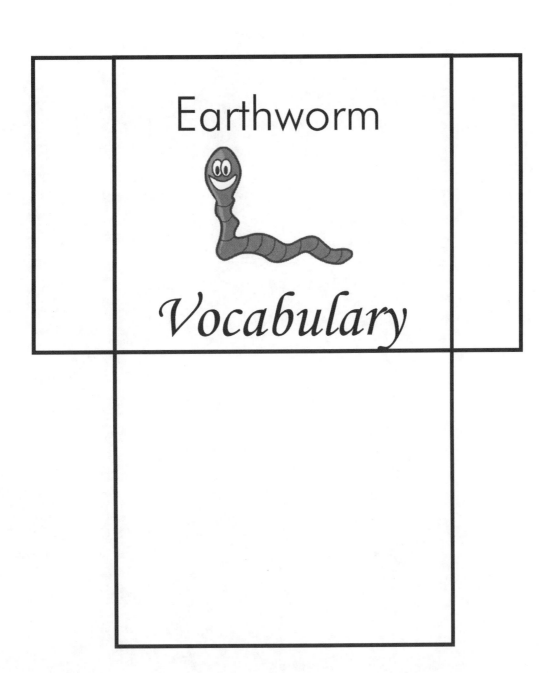

(This page left intentionally blank)

burrow

castings

cocoon

segment

(This page left intentionally blank)

setae

waste products of a worm's digestion

a hole in the ground that's been made by an animal

Zoology
Levels 1-4

(This page left intentionally blank)

where a worm's
egg grows

divisions of an
earthworm's
body that helps
it move

small bristles on
each of an
earthworm's
segments

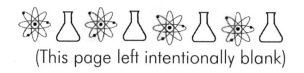

(This page left intentionally blank)

Worm Tunnels

Cut around the outside of the first circle, as well as along the dotted lines to cut out the "cut out here" section. Cut around the outside of the second circle. Stack the first circle on the second circle and secure with a brad. Read about worm tunnels and how they benefit the soil and plants.

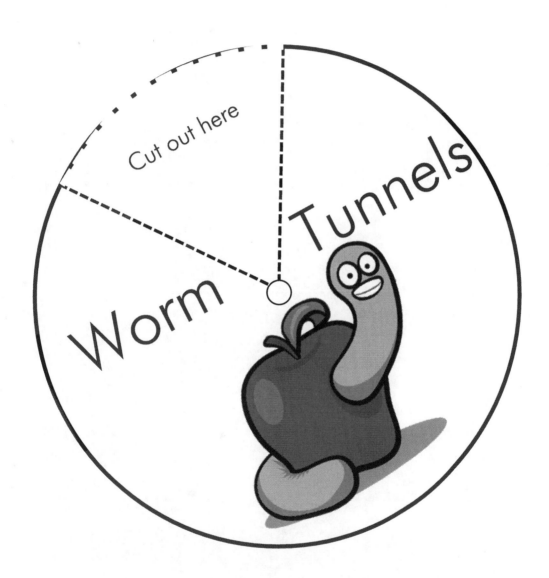

(This page left intentionally blank)

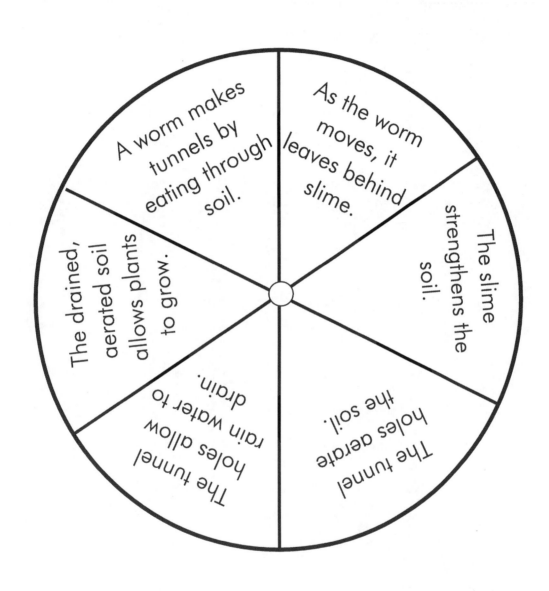

(This page left intentionally blank)

Worm Movement

Cut the piece out in full and fold on the dotted line. Inside the book (opposite "glue here"), answer the question.

(glue here)

How does a worm move?

(This page left intentionally blank)

Worm Reproduction

Cut out the rectangle as one piece and fold on the center line. Cut on the dotted line to the center fold. Inside write or paste the facts.

(glue here)

Mating

Hatching

Worms mate on warm, damp nights.

The worm makes a sticky belt of slime and lays eggs in it.

The belt become a cocoon where eggs grow.

Eggs take weeks to months to grow in the cocoon.

Some eggs don't survive.

The eggs hatch and the worms can live 10 or more years.

Zoology
Levels 1-4

(This page left intentionally blank)

Zoology
Levels 1-4

Earthworm Enemies

Lesson
95

Cut out the rectangle as one piece. Fold the left side in (on the line at A), and fold the right side in (on the line at B). Cut on the dotted lines so that each animal is a strip you can open to the fold. On the inside (opposite "glue here"), write or paste the enemy information.

bird

hedgehog

mole

shrew

A →

(glue here)

↓ B

Earthworm Enemies

Zoology
Levels 1-4

(This page left intentionally blank)

Shrews eat while worms are active at night.

Moles eat worms while they tunnel through the ground.

Hedgehogs eat while worms are active at night.

Birds eat worms mainly in the spring.

(This page left intentionally blank)

Worm Food

Cut the big rectangle as one piece and fold the outside squares in to the middle. Glue the label pieces on top of the folded piece. Inside, write or paste the various examples of worm food.

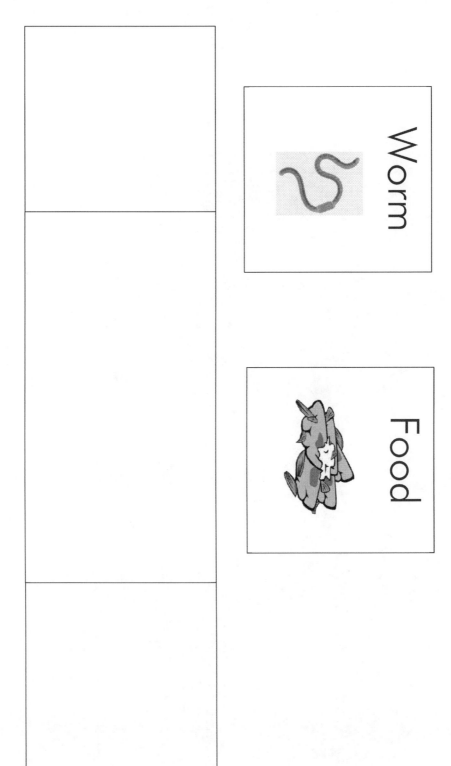

(This page left intentionally blank)

carrots

banana peels

decaying plants

potato peels

celery

orange rinds

egg shells

cabbage

tea bags

(This page left intentionally blank)

Worm Anatomy

Cut out the rectangle as one piece and fold on the dotted line. Inside, write or paste the information about a worm's body.

Worm Body

A worm body is segmented and covered with bristles.

A worm doesn't have eyes or ears.

A worm breathes through its skin and doesn't have lungs.

The front of the worm is the pointier end.

A worm's skin is wet.

Zoology
Levels 1-4

(This page left intentionally blank)

Worm Anatomy

Cut the big rectangle as one piece and fold the outside squares in to the middle.
Glue the label pieces on top of the folded piece. Paste into your lapbook.

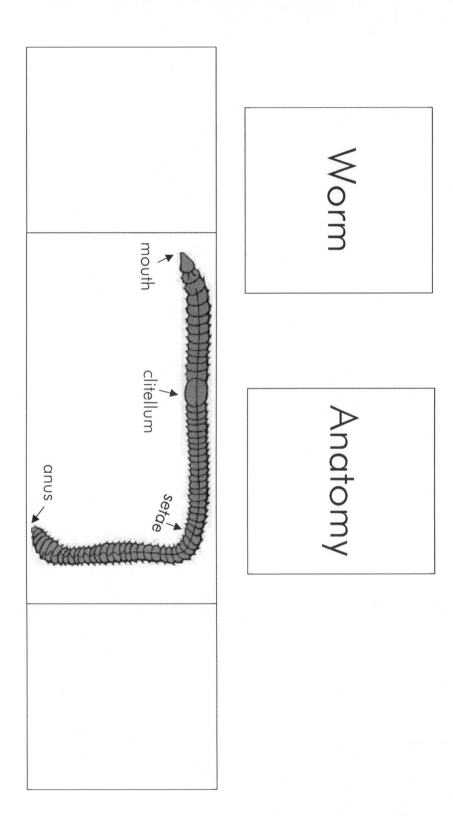

Worm

Anatomy

(This page left intentionally blank)

Dig In!

Cut out the rectangle as one piece and fold on the dotted line. Inside, write or paste the information about how a worm digs in to the ground to avoid capture.

Dig In!

When a bird (or child or anything else) tries to pull a worm out of the ground, a worm uses it **setae** — those bristles on each of its segments — to sort of grab onto the sides of its burrow, making it difficult to pull out of the ground.

(This page left intentionally blank)

Worm Facts

Cut out the hexagons and stack them with the "cover" piece on top. Write interesting worm facts on each piece. Staple and add to your lapbook.

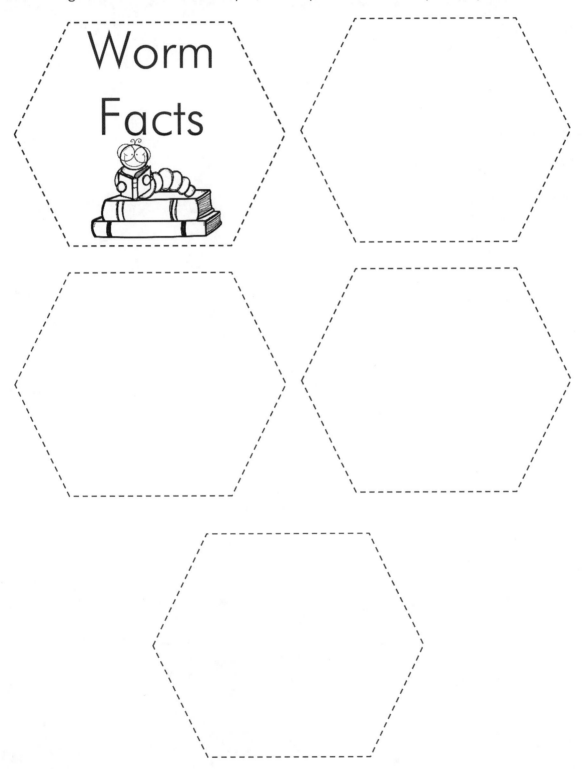

Worm
Facts

(This page left intentionally blank)

Ocean Zone Bingo

This page is your bingo board. Instructions for adding the pieces are on the next page. Use coins, small toys, paper clips – any kind of small marker that you can find. Mark off each space as it's called. You can get bingo by getting three in a row in any direction.

Ocean Zone Bingo

Sunlight Zone			
Twilight Zone			
Midnight Zone			

(This page left intentionally blank)

Ocean Zone Bingo

Cut the pieces one row at a time so you don't lose track of where they belong. The top row is the sunlight zone – shuffle them and place them on the top row of your bingo board in random order. The second row is the twilight zone. The third is the midnight zone. There is an extra animal for each zone for variation purposes. The next page is for the "caller."

jellyfish	rays	seaweed	whales
octopus	small crustaceans	viper fish	squid
brittle star	clam	crab	sea cucumber

(This page left intentionally blank)

Ocean Zone Bingo

This page is for the "caller." Cut out and mix up all of the pieces. Draw them one at a time from a stack or a bag and have players mark them off their boards as they're called.

jellyfish	rays	seaweed	whales
octopus	small crustaceans	viper fish	squid
brittle star	clam	crab	sea cucumber

(This page left intentionally blank)

Ocean Zones

Use the information about ocean zones to answer the questions.

This zone gets the most sunlight, so plants, such as seaweed, abound. Some common animals of the sunlit zone would be seals, sea turtles, sea lions, manta rays, whales, jellyfish, and sharks.

Sunlit Zone
0-656 feet

A small amount of light reaches the twilight zone, so no plants grow. Octopuses and squid and small crustaceans can be found in this zone.

Twilight Zone
656-3,280 feet

The midnight zone doesn't get any sunlight at all. Some of the animals in this zone don't even have eyes. Anglerfish, snipe eel, and tripod fish can be found in this zone.

Midnight Zone
3,280-13,123 feet

The abyss includes sea creatures that don't have a backbone such as sea spiders. Blind shrimp and hagfish can also be found in the abyss.

Abyss
13,123-19,685 feet

The hadal zone mostly includes frigid parts of the ocean in deep canyons and trenches. Despite the depths and the cold, some life can be found in the hadal zone, including sea cucumbers.

Hadal Zone
19,685-36,197 feet

(This page left intentionally blank)

Ocean Zones

Use the information about ocean zones to answer the questions.

Which ocean zone only gets dim light?

O Sunlit zone   O Twilight Zone   O Midnight Zone   O Abyss   O Hadal Zone

What zone would you be in if you were at 14,000 feet?

O Sunlit zone   O Twilight Zone   O Midnight Zone   O Abyss   O Hadal Zone

Which ocean zone is the deepest?

O Sunlit zone   O Twilight Zone   O Midnight Zone   O Abyss   O Hadal Zone

Which ocean zone gets the most sun light?

O Sunlit zone   O Twilight Zone   O Midnight Zone   O Abyss   O Hadal Zone

Which ocean zone includes plants?

O Sunlit zone   O Twilight Zone   O Midnight Zone   O Abyss   O Hadal Zone

In which ocean zone might you find an anglerfish?

O Sunlit zone   O Twilight Zone   O Midnight Zone   O Abyss   O Hadal Zone

(This page left intentionally blank)

All
About
Sharks

(This page left intentionally blank)

What is a Shark?

Cut out the rectangle as one piece and fold on the dotted line. Inside (opposite the "glue here" side), write or paste the information about sharks.

(glue here)

What is a Shark?

A shark is the fastest **fish** in the ocean. The temperature of the water determines a shark's body temperature because they are **cold-blooded**. Like other fish, they breathe with **gills**. There are more than 250 species of sharks!

(This page left intentionally blank)

Vocabulary

Cut out the beach cards. Write the word from the box that best fits the definition.
Stack the cards into a book with the title page on top and add to your lapbook.

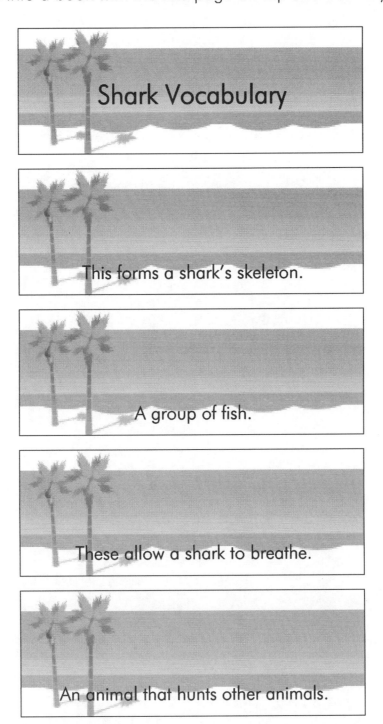

Shark Vocabulary

This forms a shark's skeleton.

A group of fish.

These allow a shark to breathe.

An animal that hunts other animals.

| gills | cartilage | school | predator |

(This page left intentionally blank)

Shark Sizes

Use the information at the bottom to fill in the graph on shark sizes. Cut out the chart and add to your lapbook.

	Bull	Great White	Leopard	Nurse	Thresher	Whale
60 feet						
55 feet						
50 feet						
45 feet						
40 feet						
35 feet						
30 feet						
25 feet						
20 feet						
15 feet						
10 feet						
5 feet						

Bull shark – 12 feet long

Great White shark – 24 feet long

Leopard shark – 7 feet long

Nurse shark – 14 feet long

Thresher shark – 20 feet long

Whale shark – 60 feet long

(This page left intentionally blank)

Types of Sharks

Cut out each piece and stack them in size order (cover on top, longest piece on bottom). Write or paste the information about each type of shark.

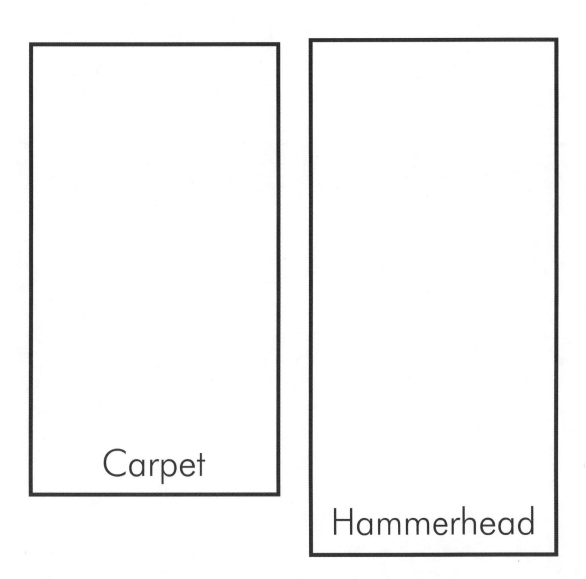

Carpet

Hammerhead

(This page left intentionally blank)

Mackerel

Requiem

(This page left intentionally blank)

Types of sharks

Carpet Sharks

Some types of carpet sharks are nurse sharks and whale sharks.

Hammerhead Sharks

This is the third largest family of sharks. Some types are bonnetheads and great hammer-heads.

Requiem Sharks

This is the largest of the shark families. Some examples of this family are tiger, leopard, and bull sharks.

Mackerel Sharks

Mackerel sharks are the second largest family of sharks and include such sharks as the mako and great white varieties.

(This page left intentionally blank)

Shark Anatomy

Cut out the labeled shark and glue into the middle rectangle of the piece on the left. Cut as one piece and fold the outside squares to cover the shark. Glue the label pieces on top of the folded piece.

Shark Anatomy

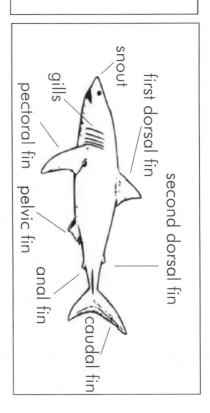

snout

first dorsal fin

gills

second dorsal fin

pectoral fin

pelvic fin

anal fin

caudal fin

(This page left intentionally blank)

Shark Anatomy

Cut each piece out in full (don't cut off the tab label). Write or glue information on each piece. Stack the pieces so the tabs are in order from left to right with the cover page on top.

Parts of a Shark

Denticles

The scales that cover a shark's skin are called denticles. They protect from bites and scratches.

1

Dorsal Fin

The dorsal fin is the shark's large fin. It is what keeps the shark from rolling over in the water.

2

(This page left intentionally blank)

Pectoral Fin

The pectoral fin is what the shark uses to move up and down in the water.

3

Caudal Fin

The caudal fin – the tail of the shark – is how the shark pushes itself through the water.

4

Eyes

A shark can move its eyes to see in different directions. Some species have protective membranes over their eyes.

5

(This page left intentionally blank)

Shark Hunting and Teeth

Cut out the rectangles and fold on the dotted line. Inside (opposite the "glue here" side), write or glue the information about how sharks use their senses to hunt and facts about shark teeth.

(glue here)

Mighty Hunter

(glue here)

Shark Teeth

(This page left intentionally blank)

Sound waves travel far and help sharks hear prey moving through the water. They can sense movement and even detect electrical impulses. Sharks can see, but they are colorblind. They can pre-taste food by bumping into it with their snouts. Sharks can smell things from a long way away. They are especially attracted to blood.

Sharks don't use their teeth to chew, but rather to tear their food. They swallow huge chunks without chewing. The process of tearing their food causes sharks to lose several teeth each time they eat. This is no problem for a shark, though! They have up to 7 rows of teeth. When a tooth falls out of one row, the tooth behind it moves into its place.

(This page left intentionally blank)

Where Do Sharks Live?

Cut out the hexagons and stack them with the title page on top. Staple and add to your lapbook.

Where do sharks live?

Some live along coastlines.

Some live in deep water.

Some live in salt water.

Some live in fresh water.

(This page left intentionally blank)

Shark Diet

Cut out the rectangle as one piece and fold on the dotted line. Inside (opposite the "glue here" side), write or paste what a shark eats.

(glue here)

Shark Diet

Sharks will eat almost anything they can find, but their preferences are fish, crab, shrimp, squid, and octopus. They hunt alone or in groups.

(This page left intentionally blank)

Shark Relatives

Cut out the rectangle as one piece and fold on the dotted line. Inside (opposite the "glue here" side), write or paste about shark relatives.

(glue here)

Shark Relatives

Sharks are related to other animals with skeletons made of cartilage, including skates and rays. Their official name is elasmobranches.

(This page left intentionally blank)

Baby Shark Do Do Doo...

Cut out the rectangle as one piece and fold on the dotted line. Inside (opposite the "glue here" side), write or paste information about baby sharks.

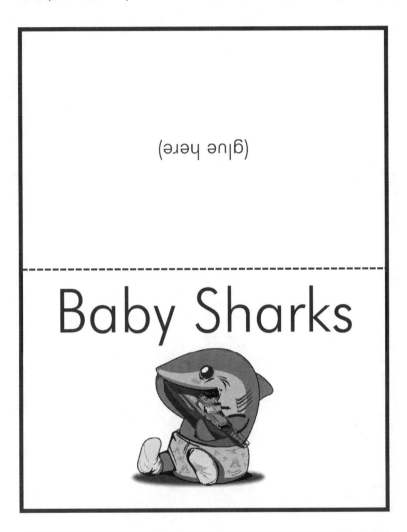

(glue here)

Baby Sharks

Some shark species lay eggs. Other mothers carry their babies (called pups) inside their body for anywhere from 10 months to 2 years. A mother can have up to 48 pups in her lifetime! Young sharks mostly eat small fish and shrimp.

(This page left intentionally blank)

Shark Species

Cut out as one piece. Fold up bottom. Then fold back side tabs and secure to the back flap. You have made a pocket to hold the species cards in your lapbook. Cut out the species cards and glue the information onto the word card. (The information goes in the order the sharks are presented starting with great white.) Store the word cards in the pocket.

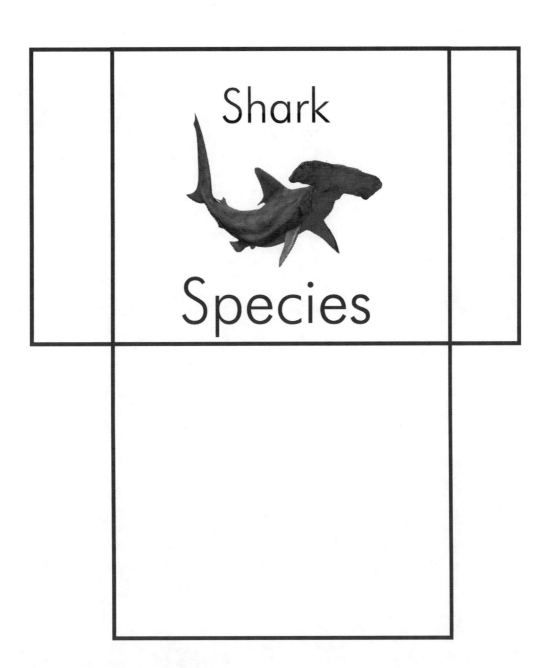

(This page left intentionally blank)

great white

hammerhead

tiger

nurse

(This page left intentionally blank)

✳ ⚗ ✳ ⚗ ✳ ⚗ ✳ ⚗

whale

These sharks have been found in all oceans and in both deep and shallow water. They eat fish, dolphins, other sharks, and even the bodies of dead whales. They sneak attack from behind and below.

These sharks live in warm, shallow water, swimming north in the summer and south in the winter. Hammerheads eat small fish, stingrays, crustaceans, and other sharks. They usually hunt at night.

(This page left intentionally blank)

These sharks are usually found in deep waters near coral reefs. They eat most anything (even license plates, tin cans, and people!) but also lobster, squid, fish, sea turtles, birds and smaller sharks.

These sharks live in shallow water. They like to stay in dark places during the day. They eat at night, preferring crabs, shrimp, lobster, sea urchins, and fish.

These sharks are the largest fish in the world. They are found in warm oceans. They swim with their mouths open and scoop up plankton, shrimp, and small fish.

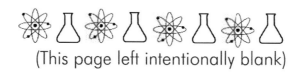

(This page left intentionally blank)

Helping and Hurting

Cut out the rectangle as one piece and fold on the center line. Cut on the dotted line to the center fold. Inside (opposite the "glue here" side), write or glue the information.

(glue here)

How Sharks Help | How Sharks are Hurt

(This page left intentionally blank)

Sharks help keep the ocean healthy by eating sick or dead animals. Some experts are researching sharks' bodies for the potential they might hold to help cure cancer.

At least 100 million sharks are caught each year for sport or for their meat. They are also killed for their skin and their fins. Of course some sharks are killed in accidents with boats or by getting caught in fishing nets.

(This page left intentionally blank)

Critter Cards

Learn the names of these critters. Cut them out. Ask someone to play with you. Have the person pick one card. You ask yes and no questions to figure out which critter it is. They can only answer you yes or no. Do all the cards.

squid

clam

sea urchin

sea star

sea otter

sea anemone

(This page left intentionally blank)

All
About
Jellyfish

(This page left intentionally blank)

What and Where

Cut out the rectangles and fold on the dotted line. Inside (opposite the "glue here" side), write or paste about jellyfish classification and where they're found in the world.

(glue here)

What is a Jellyfish?

(glue here)

Where are jellyfish found?

Jellyfish aren't actually fish. They are cnidarians — a group of soft, boneless sea animals. Cnidarians are one of the most common groups of sea animals, and include corals, freshwater hydras, and sea anemones.

Jellyfish are found in every ocean in the world, even including the icy waters!

(This page left intentionally blank)

Movement

Cut out the rectangle as one piece and fold on the dotted line. Inside (opposite the "glue here" side), write or paste the information about how jellyfish move.

(glue here)

How do jellyfish move?

Jellyfish move by contracting their bodies, forcing the water inside of them out and propelling them forward. Currents and winds usually determine the path a jellyfish follows, which is why so many wash up on shorelines.

(This page left intentionally blank)

Anatomy

Cut out the rectangle as one piece and fold on the dotted line. Inside (opposite the "glue here" side), write or paste the information about jellyfish anatomy.

(glue here)

Jellyfish
Anatomy

Jellyfish are mostly just a stomach. They don't have any bones, eyes, or even a brain. They don't have lungs or gills, but rather absorb oxygen through their skin. They do have mouths in the middle of the underside of their bell-shaped top. Many jellyfish also have tentacles.

(This page left intentionally blank)

Jellyfish Size

Cut out the rectangle as one piece and fold on the center line. Cut on the dotted line to the center fold. Inside (opposite the "glue here" side), write or paste the information about jellyfish size.

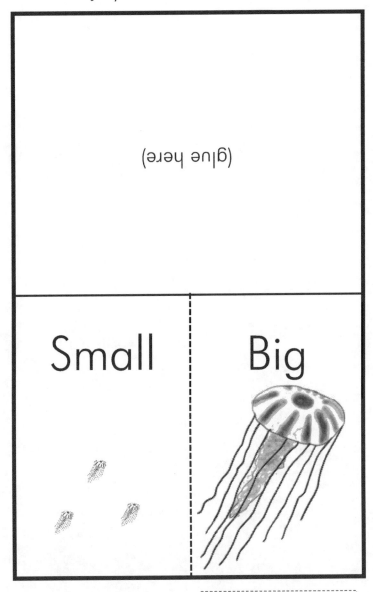

(glue here)

Small | Big

The smallest jellyfish are only about the size of a fingernail!

The largest jellyfish are up to eight feet wide and 100 feet long!

(This page left intentionally blank)

Jellyfish Life Cycle

Cut around the outside of the first circle, as well as along the dotted lines to cut out the "cut out here" section. Cut around the outside of the second circle. Stack the first circle on the second circle and secure with a brad.

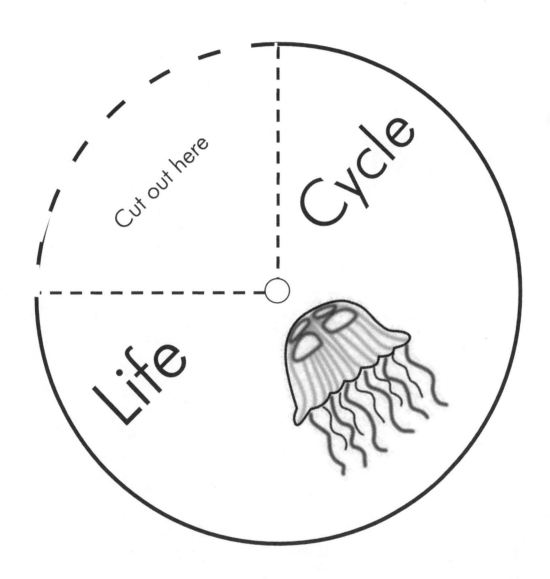

(This page left intentionally blank)

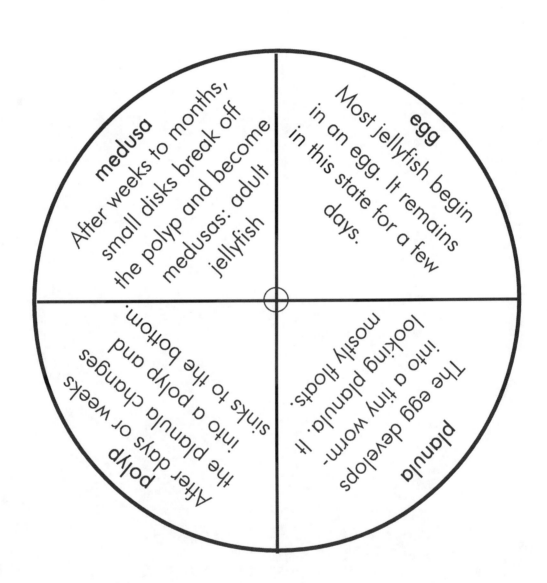

egg
Most jellyfish begin in an egg. It remains in this state for a few days.

medusa
After weeks to months, small disks break off the polyp and become medusas: adult jellyfish

planula
The egg develops into a tiny worm-looking planula. It mostly floats.

polyp
After days or weeks the planula changes into a polyp and sinks to the bottom.

(This page left intentionally blank)

Diet

Cut out the rectangle as one piece and fold on the dotted line. Inside (opposite the "glue here" side), write or paste the information about jellyfish diet.

(glue here)

Jellyfish
Diet

Jellyfish don't really have to hunt. They wait for small animals to swim into their tentacles. Animals such as zooplankton, small fish, and even other jellyfish are the typical diet.

(This page left intentionally blank)

Tentacles

Cut out the piece as one and fold in half at the head. Write or paste about jellyfish tentacles inside.

Jellyfish tentacles are filled with stinging cells. When something brushes against them, the cells explode and emit toxins. This paralyzes the prey and the jellyfish are free to eat.

(This page left intentionally blank)

Predators and Protection

Cut each piece out in full and fold each piece on the dotted line. Write or paste the applicable information inside its small piece, then glue the two small pieces into the large piece. Glue the large piece into your lapbook (on the "glue here" side).

(glue here)

Predators and Protection

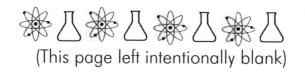

(This page left intentionally blank)

Predators

Many animals are immune to the sting of a jellyfish. Sea turtles, crabs, some birds, sea snails, and some kinds of fish prey on jellyfish. There are even humans who eat them!

Box jellyfish kill more people than sharks do. A sting from a jellyfish can kill a person within minutes. In addition to stinging tentacles as offense, jellyfish can use their transparency to hide from predators in defense.

Protection

(This page left intentionally blank)

Vocabulary Matching

Cut out the cards and mix them up. Match the word to its definition in a "memory match" game. Store the cards in the pocket in your lapbook. Each word starts beside its match so study them before cutting them out.

bell	The umbrella-shaped top of a jellyfish	current	The flow of water; determines where a jellyfish moves.
invertebrate	An animal without a backbone.	predator	An animal that eats other animals.
smack	A group of jellyfish.	tentacles	The long, arm-like body parts that grow from the bell of a jellyfish.
toxin	A harmful substance.	transparent	Clear; see through

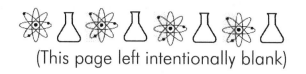

(This page left intentionally blank)

Vocabulary Matching Pocket

Cut out as one piece. Fold up bottom. Then fold back side tabs and secure to the back flap. You have made a pocket to hold the vocabulary matching cards in your lapbook.

Jellyfish
Vocabulary
Cards

(This page left intentionally blank)

All
About
Whales

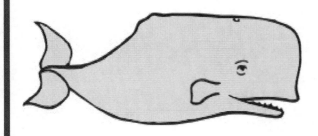

(This page left intentionally blank)

Classification of Whales

Cut out the rectangle as one piece. Fold the left side in (on the line at **A**), and fold the right side in (on the line at **B**). Cut on the dotted lines so that there are 4 strips you can open to the fold. On the inside (opposite "glue here"), write the classification of whales: kingdom – Animalia; phylum – Chordata; Class – Mammalia; order – Cetacea.

Kingdom

Phylum

Class

Order

A

(glue here)

B

Classification of Whales

(This page left intentionally blank)

Whale Anatomy

Cut around the outside of the first circle, as well as along the dotted lines to cut out the "cut out here" section. Cut around the outside of the second circle. Stack the first circle on the second circle and secure with a brad. Learn from the wheel what all whales, whether toothed or baleen, have.

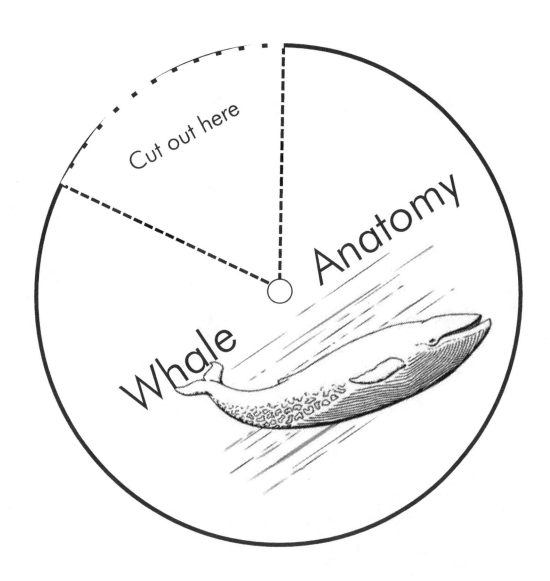

Cut out here

Whale Anatomy

(This page left intentionally blank)

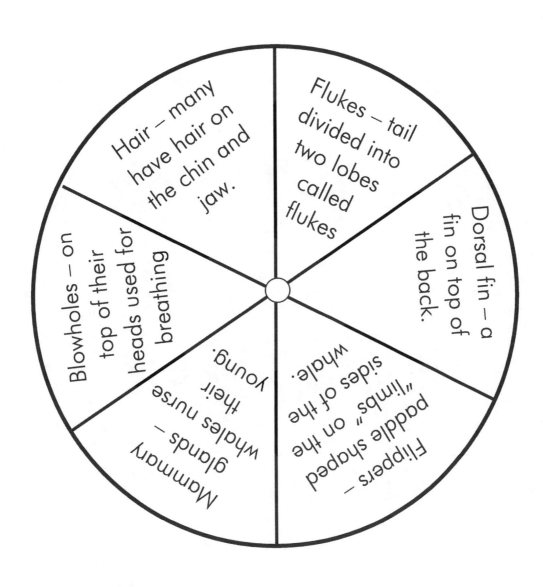

Hair — many have hair on the chin and jaw.

Flukes — tail divided into two lobes called flukes

Dorsal fin — a fin on top of the back.

Blowholes — on top of their heads used for breathing

Mammary glands — whales nurse their young.

Flippers — paddle shaped "limbs" on the sides of the whale.

Zoology
Levels 1-4

(This page left intentionally blank)

Whale Sizes

Use the information at the bottom to fill in the graph on whale sizes. Cut out the chart and add to your lapbook.

	Beluga	Blue	Bowhead	Gray	Humpback	Orca	Sperm
90 feet							
85 feet							
80 feet							
75 feet							
70 feet							
65 feet							
60 feet							
55 feet							
50 feet							
45 feet							
40 feet							
35 feet							
30 feet							
25 feet							
20 feet							
15 feet							
10 feet							
5 feet							

Beluga – 15 feet

Blue – 80-90 feet

Bowhead 50-60 feet

Gray 45-50 feet

Humpback – 52 feet

Orca – 27-33 feet

Sperm – 50-60 feet

Zoology
Levels 1-4

(This page left intentionally blank)

Whale Species

Cut out as one piece. Fold up bottom. Then fold back side tabs and secure to the back flap. You have made a pocket to hold the species cards in your lapbook. Cut out the species cards and glue the information onto the word card. (The information goes in the order the whales are presented starting with orca.) Store the word cards in the pocket.

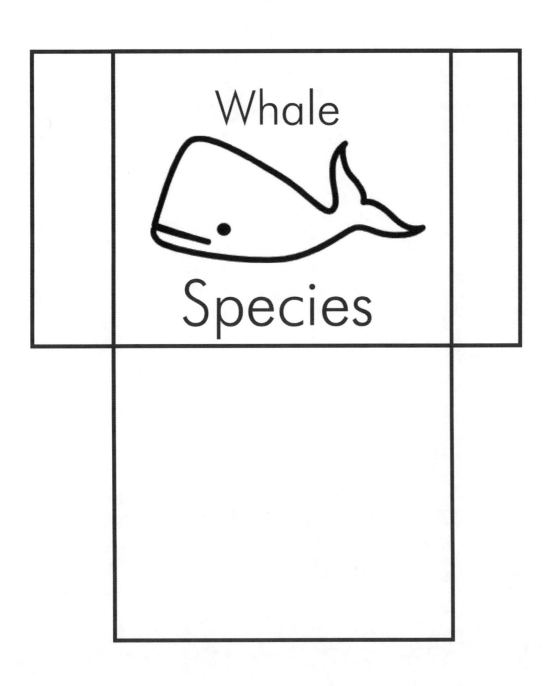

(This page left intentionally blank)

orca

sperm whale

beluga

blue whale

(This page left intentionally blank)

humback

Orcas are toothed whales. They eat hundreds of pounds of food each day! They live in close-knit pods and are the largest of the dolphin family. Orcas can swim in bursts over 30 mph.

Sperm whales are the largest toothed whales and have the biggest brain of any animal. They live in close-knit pods. They inhabit deep, offshore waters of most oceans. They produce a valuable oil in their large heads.

(This page left intentionally blank)

A beluga is a small, toothed whale. These are very sociable whales and live in large pods. They live in arctic waters and migrate in the spring. Mother and calf form a strong bond and often return to the same summer spot.

Blue whales are the largest baleen whales. Fifty people could stand on a blue whale's tongue alone! They are the loudest animal on earth. They live near the surface of all the oceans in the world.

Humpbacks are also baleen whales. They communicate by "singing." They hunt using bubble-net feeding by forming a circle with the rest of the pod, blowing a wall of bubbles, and trapping small fish, krill, etc.

(This page left intentionally blank)

Blubber

Cut out the rectangle as one piece and fold on the dotted line. Inside (opposite the "glue here" side), write facts about blubber.

(This page left intentionally blank)

Migration

Use different colors to mark the migration routes of different whales. Be sure to make a key. Cut out the map and key and put them in your lapbook.

Key

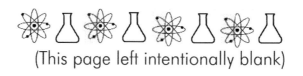

(This page left intentionally blank)

Whale Tricks

Cut out each piece and stack them in size order (cover on top, longest piece on bottom). Write or paste about the trick on each piece.

Whale
tricks

"Jumping" high and
slapping the water

breaching

lobtailing

(This page left intentionally blank)

spyhopping

logging

Sticking the tail out of the water, swinging it around, then slapping the water with it.

Poking the head out and turning around like they're "spying."

Floating at the surface with part of the head or back showing above the water.

(This page left intentionally blank)

Vocabulary

Write the word from the box that best fits the definition onto the whales. Stack and staple them and add them to your lapbook.

| baleen | echolocation | melon | migrate | pod |

Whale Vocabulary

How toothed whales navigate by sending out a sound and allowing it to bounce back.

A family of whales.

Move from one place to another.

A sieve-like part that filters plankton from the water.

A fat-filled organ in the whale's head.

(This page left intentionally blank)

Compare and Contrast

Cut out the rectangle as one piece and fold on the center line. Cut on the dotted line to the center fold. Inside (opposite the "glue here" side), compare and contrast baleen and toothed whales.

(glue here)

Baleen whales

Toothed whales

(This page left intentionally blank)

Whale Extremes

Cut out the rectangles and fold on the dotted line. Inside (opposite the "glue here" side), write what you know about whale extremes. What is the largest whale? The smallest? The loudest? Use your whale cards and do further research if needed.

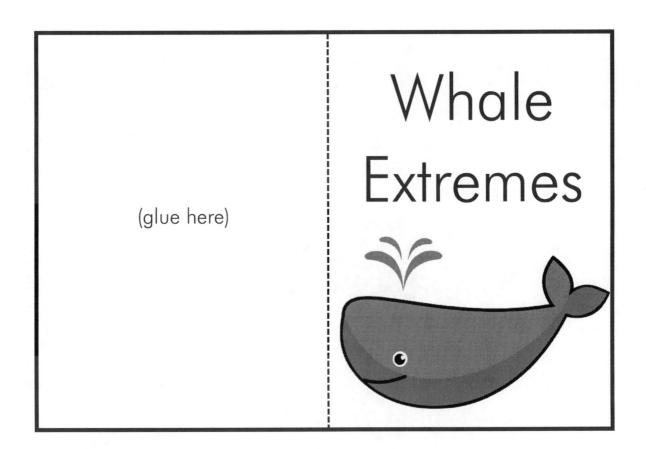

(glue here)

Whale Extremes

(This page left intentionally blank)

Cattle Types

Can you match the different cattle names with their description? Learn from the answer key if you don't know which is which.

a. bull

b. calf

c. cow

d. heifer

e. herd

f. oxen

g. steer

____ young cattle

____ female cattle before giving birth

____ female cattle after giving birth

____ male cattle

____ group of cattle

____ male cattle raised for beef

____ large, heavy male cattle raised for work

(This page left intentionally blank)

Cattle Products and Uses

List some cattle products and uses.

_____

_____

_____

_____

_____

_____

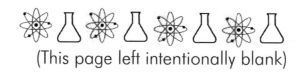

(This page left intentionally blank)

Cow Facts

Write down some interesting things you've learned about cows.

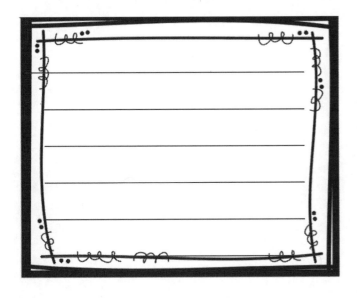

(This page left intentionally blank)

Cow Life Cycle

Cut around the outside of the first circle, as well as along the dotted lines to cut out the "cut out here" section. Cut around the outside of the second circle. Stack the first circle on the second circle and secure with a brad.

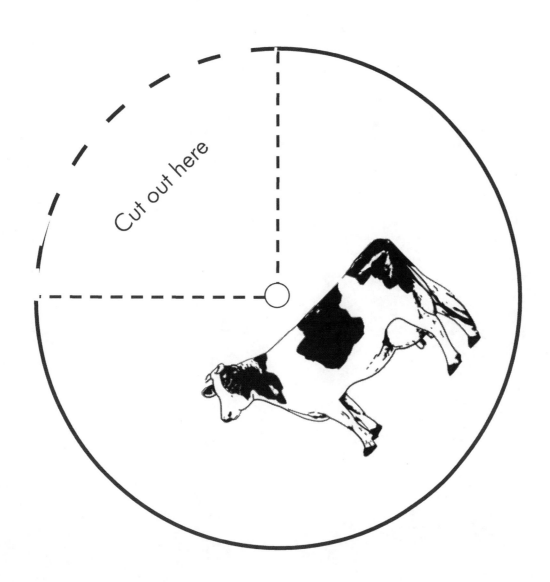

Cut out here

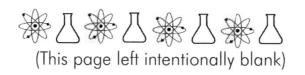

(This page left intentionally blank)

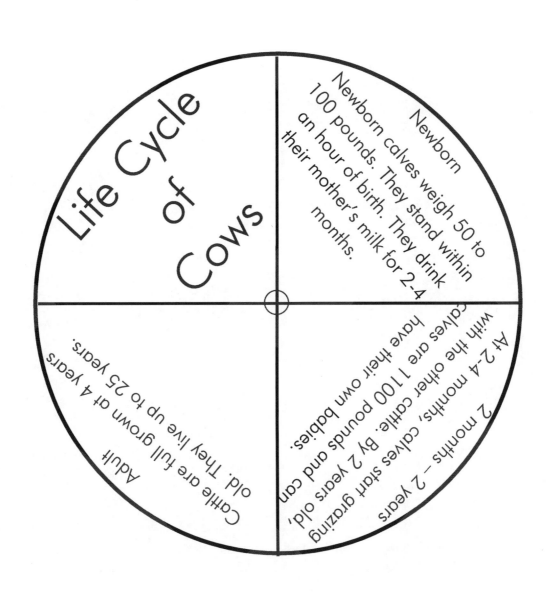

Life Cycle of Cows

Newborn
Newborn calves weigh 50 to 100 pounds. They stand within an hour of birth. They drink their mother's milk for 2-4 months.

2 months – 2 years
At 2-4 months, calves start grazing with the other cattle. By 2 years old, calves are 1100 pounds and can have their own babies.

Adult
Cattle are full grown at 4 years old. They live up to 25 years.

(This page left intentionally blank)

Vocabulary Matching

Cut out the cards and mix them up. Match the word to its definition in a "memory match" game. Store the cards in the pocket in your lapbook. Each word starts beside its match so study them before cutting them out.

calving	Cows giving birth – usually takes place in the spring	cattle drive	Ranchers ride horses beside their cattle to move them to new pastures.
cowhide	A cow's skin – used to make leather	manure	The cow's waste.
pasture	Grassy areas where cows feed	protein	Building block of cells – found in milk
silage	Cow feed made of corn or alfalfa and stored in silos.	veal	Meat of a baby cow

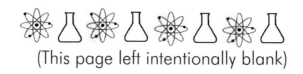

(This page left intentionally blank)

All

About

Monkeys

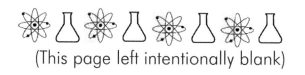

(This page left intentionally blank)

Classification of Monkeys

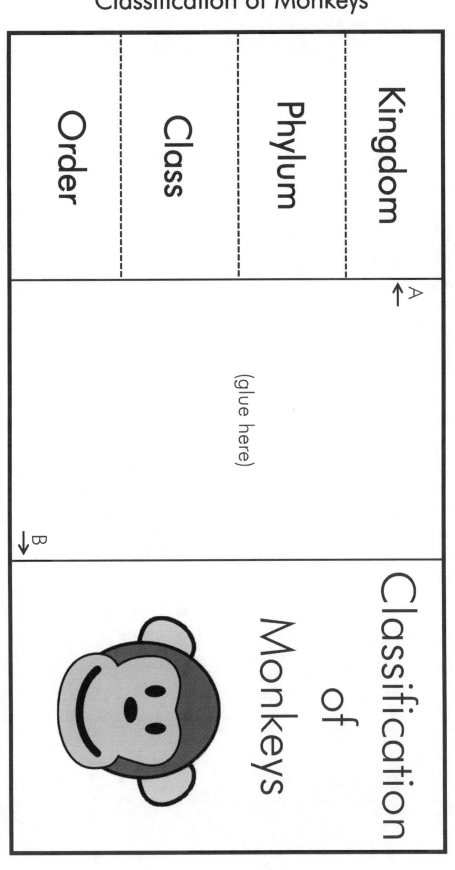

Kingdom

Phylum

Class

Order

A →

(glue here)

↓ B

Classification of Monkeys

Cut out the rectangle as one piece. Fold the left side in (on the line at **A**), and fold the right side in (on the line at **B**). Cut on the dotted lines so that there are 4 strips you can open to the fold. On the inside (opposite "glue here"), write the classification of monkeys: kingdom – Animalia; phylum – Chordata; class – Mammalia; order – Primates.

(This page left intentionally blank)

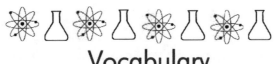

Vocabulary

Write the word from the box that best fits the definition onto the monkey heads.
Stack and staple them and add them to your lapbook.

| arboreal | chordata | prehensile | terrestrial | troop |

Monkey
Vocabulary

A group of monkeys

Living in trees

Able to grasp
things

Animals that live
mainly on land

Have a backbone

(This page left intentionally blank)

What is a Primate?

Cut out the rectangle as one piece and fold on the dotted line. Inside (opposite the "glue here" side), write or paste characteristics of primates.

(glue here)

What is a Primate?

- -

shortened snout leading to fewer teeth	clavicles resulting in enhanced shoulder motion
forward facing eyes	different types of teeth
nails instead of claws	opposable thumbs

(This page left intentionally blank)

Monkey Behavior

Cut out the shape as one piece and fold at the connection at the head. Inside (opposite the "glue here" side), write or paste behavior of monkeys.

Monkeys are extremely social creatures. They use gestures, expressions, and vocal noises to communicate. Monkeys groom one another to show affection. They grin and yawn to express anger. If a monkey is staring, he's threatening.

(This page left intentionally blank)

Monkey Locations

Cut out the map and the key. Choose two colors and color where old world monkeys are found in one color and where new world monkeys are found in the other. Be sure to mark the colors on your key. Glue the map and key into your lapbook.

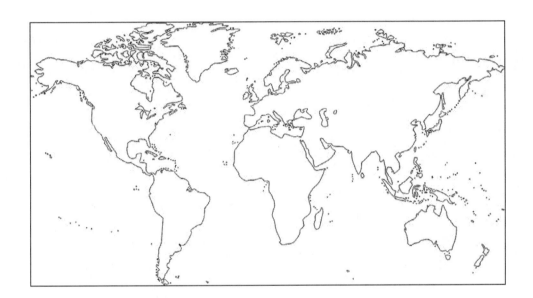

Key

☐ old world monkeys

☐ new world monkeys

(This page left intentionally blank)

Monkey Predators

Cut out the shape as one piece and fold on the dotted line. Inside, write or paste the information about monkey predators.

A monkey's predators include people, large snakes, large cats, and birds of prey. Unlike other animals that have strong defenses, monkeys use their intelligence for survival. Some monkeys serve as guards to warn their troop that danger is close by.

(This page left intentionally blank)

Monkey Diet

Cut out the bananas and write on them things that monkeys eat. Stack and staple and add to your lapbook. Some of their food choices are leaves, nuts, eggs, fruit, as well as insects, spiders, and small mammals. This makes monkeys omnivores – they eat both plants and meat.

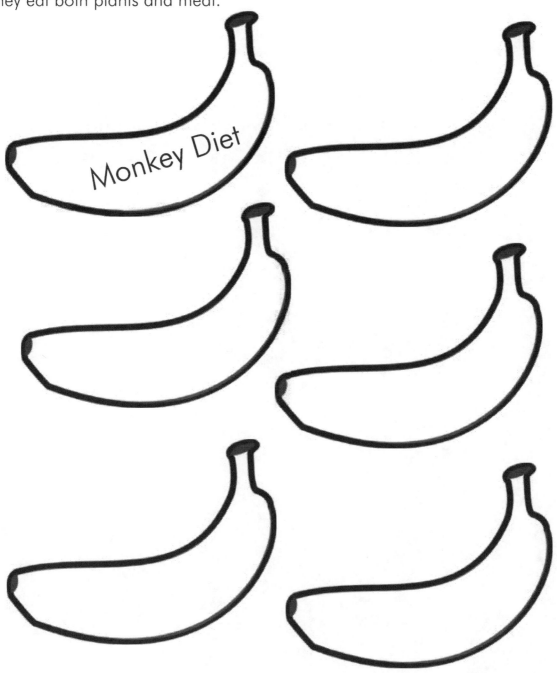

(This page left intentionally blank)

New and Old World Monkeys

Cut out the rectangle as one piece and fold on the center line. Cut on the dotted line to the center fold. Inside (opposite the "glue here" side), compare and contrast new and old world monkeys.

(glue here)

Old World
Monkeys

New World
Monkeys

(This page left intentionally blank)

Monkey Misc.

Cut out the rectangles and fold on the dotted line. Inside (opposite the "glue here" side), write or paste information about monkey babies and then any other interesting things you have learned about monkeys.

(glue here)

Monkey Babies

Monkey babies are born after a 4 to 8 month pregnancy. Like many animals, they stay with their mothers until they are weaned. Males tend to leave their mothers in adolescence. Some females never leave their mothers.

(glue here)

Fun Facts

(This page left intentionally blank)

Lapbook Pieces

Use the cards for vocabulary, sorting, matching, or other information.

(This page left intentionally blank)

Lapbook Pieces

Cut out as one piece. Fold up bottom. Then fold back side tabs and secure to the back flap. You have made a pocket to hold the cards from the previous page.

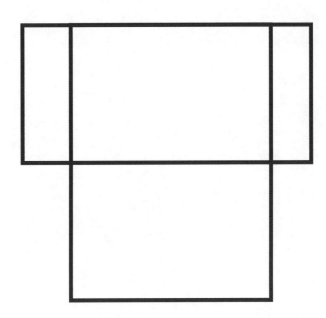

(This page left intentionally blank)

Lapbook Pieces

Cut out each piece as one and fold them in half. Write information inside. Put titles on each piece.

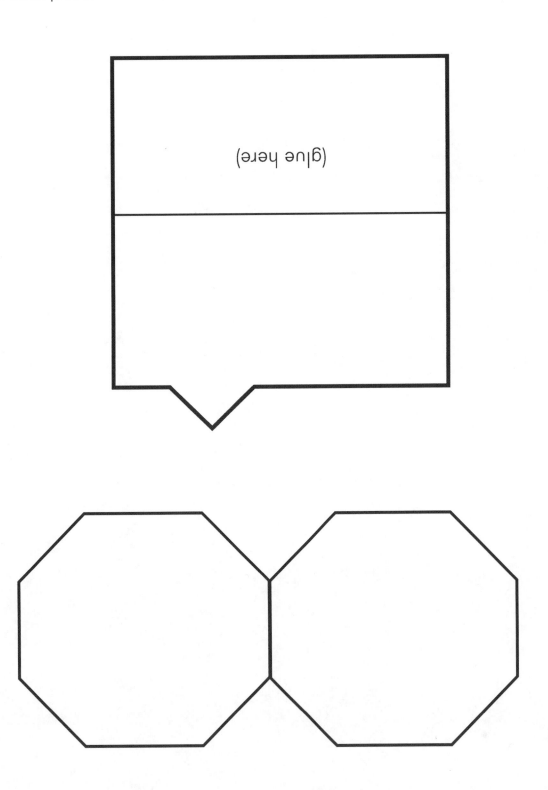

(glue here)

(This page left intentionally blank)

Lapbook pieces

↑ A

(glue here)

B ↓

Cut out the rectangle as one piece. Fold the left side in (on the line at **A**), and fold the right side in (on the line at **B**). Cut on the dotted lines so you have four strips you can label and open to the fold. On the inside (opposite "glue here"), write your information. On the right panel, create a title and add artwork if you'd like.

(This page left intentionally blank)

Lapbook pieces

Cut out the rectangle as one piece and fold on the center line. Cut on the dotted line to the center fold. Label the two flaps. Inside (opposite the "glue here" side), write your information.

(glue here)

(This page left intentionally blank)

Lapbook pieces

Cut out the rectangles and fold on the dotted line. Label the right side and add artwork if you'd like. Inside (opposite the "glue here" side), write your information.

(glue here)

(glue here)

(This page left intentionally blank)

(glue here)

(glue here)

(This page left intentionally blank)

Lapbook Pieces

A →

B →

(glue here)

Cut out the rectangle as one piece. Fold the left side in (on the line at **A**), and fold the right side in (on the line at **B**). Cut on the dotted line so that there are two strips you can open to the fold. This piece is good for comparing and contrasting or talking about two characteristics of an animal. Use the right panel to title the piece and include artwork if you want to.

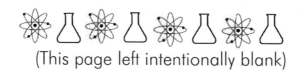

(This page left intentionally blank)

Lapbook Pieces

Cut out the hexagons. Add a title and/or artwork to one piece and information to the other pieces. Stack them and staple on the side to make a book.

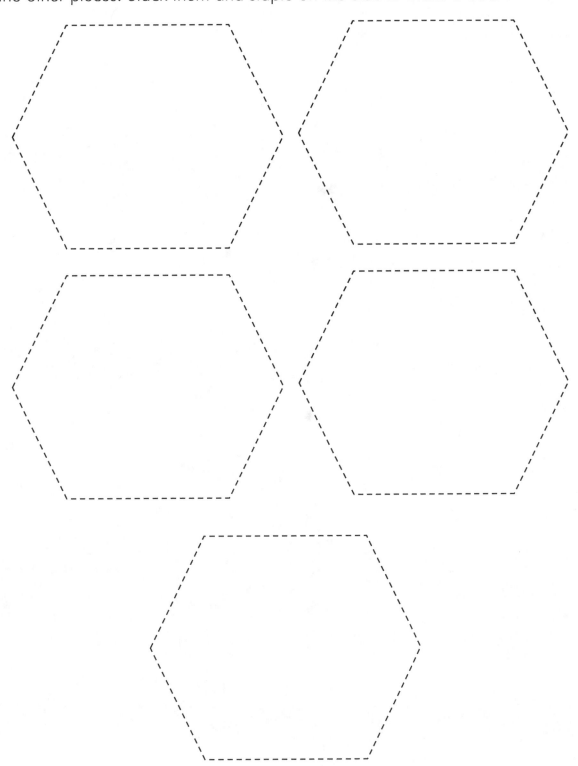

(This page left intentionally blank)

Lapbook pieces

Cut out the rectangle as one piece and fold on the dotted line. Give the piece a title and/or artwork. Inside (opposite the "glue here" side), write your information.

(glue here)

(This page left intentionally blank)

(glue here)

(This page left intentionally blank)

Lapbook Pieces

Cut out as one piece. Fold up bottom. Then fold back side tabs and secure to the back flap. Label the pocket. You have made a pocket to hold the verse cards in your lapbook. Cut out the cards. Fill in information and store them in the pocket.

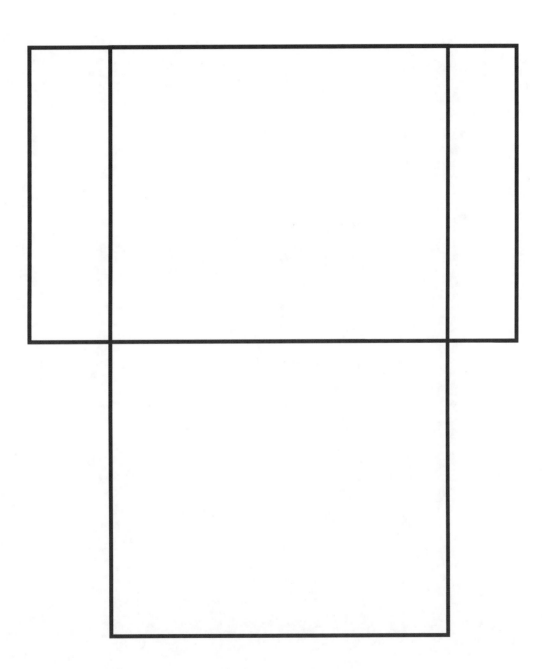

(This page left intentionally blank)

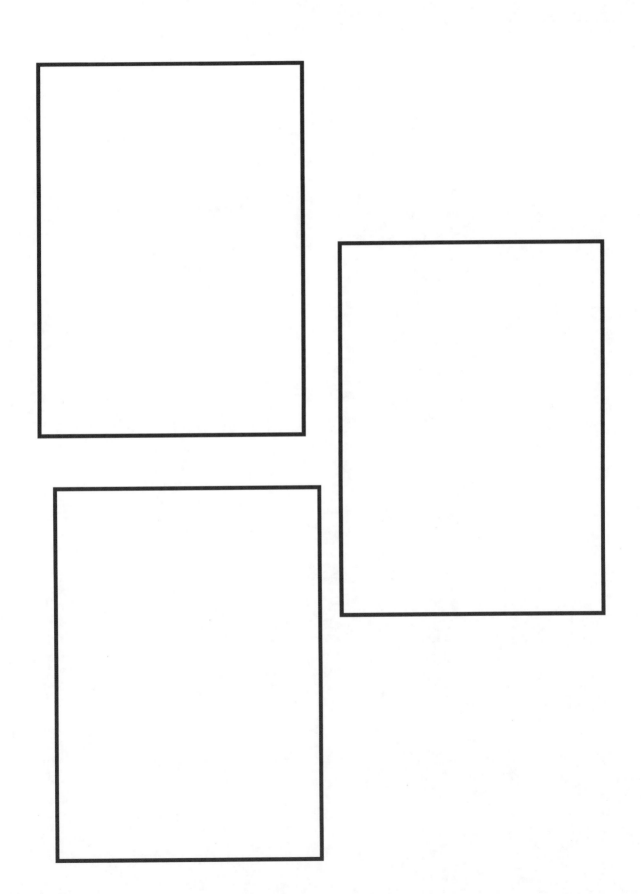

(This page left intentionally blank)

Lapbook pieces

Cut each piece out in full (don't cut off the tab label). The piece without the tab is the cover – add a title and/or artwork. Be sure to label each tab and stack them in order: cover, left tab, center tab, right tab.

(This page left intentionally blank)

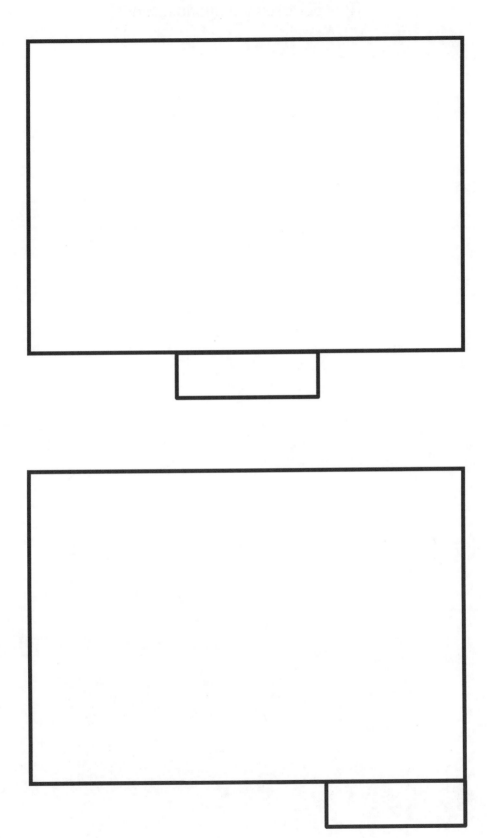

(This page left intentionally blank)

Lapbook Pieces

Cut out each piece and stack them in size order (shortest piece on top, longest piece on bottom). Label the bottom of each piece and fill in information.

(This page left intentionally blank)

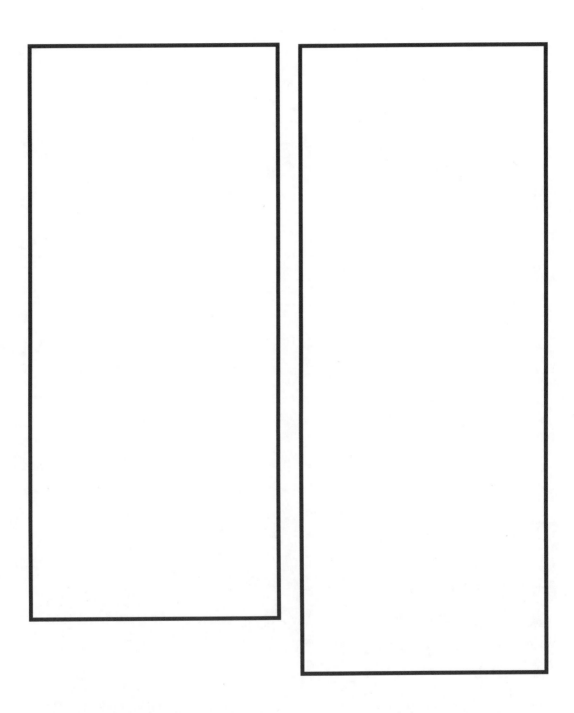

(This page left intentionally blank)

Lapbook Pieces

Cut each piece out in full and fold each piece on the dotted line. Write a title on the big book. Give each small book a topic and put facts inside. Glue the three small pieces side by side inside of the large piece.

(glue here)

(This page left intentionally blank)

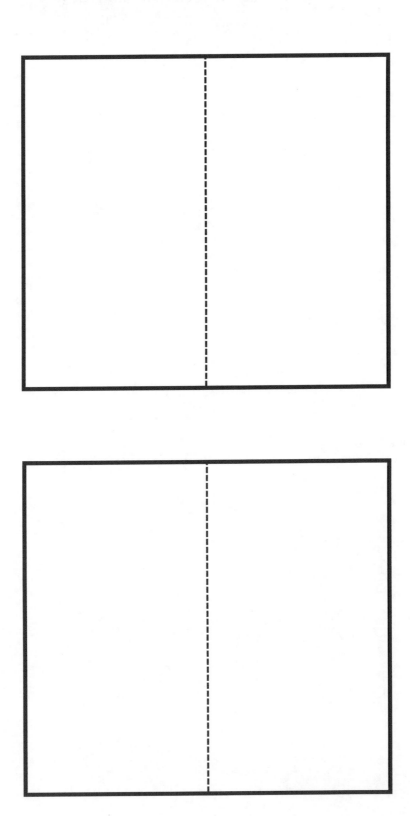

(This page left intentionally blank)

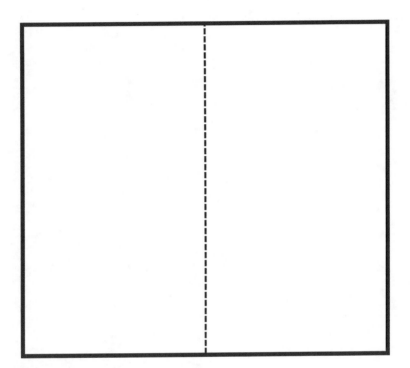

(This page left intentionally blank)

Lapbook pieces

Cut around the outside of the first circle, as well as along the dotted lines to cut out the "cut out here" section. Put a title and/or artwork on this circle. Cut around the outside of the second circle. Fill each wedge of the circle with a fact (you can add more artwork if you have too many wedges). Stack the first circle on the second circle and secure with a brad.

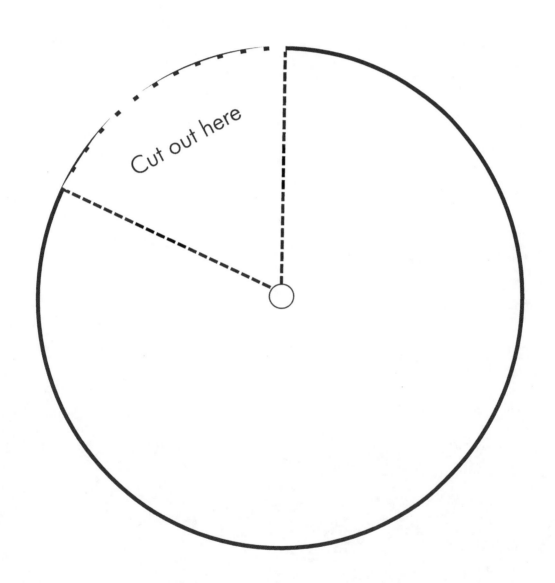

Cut out here

(This page left intentionally blank)

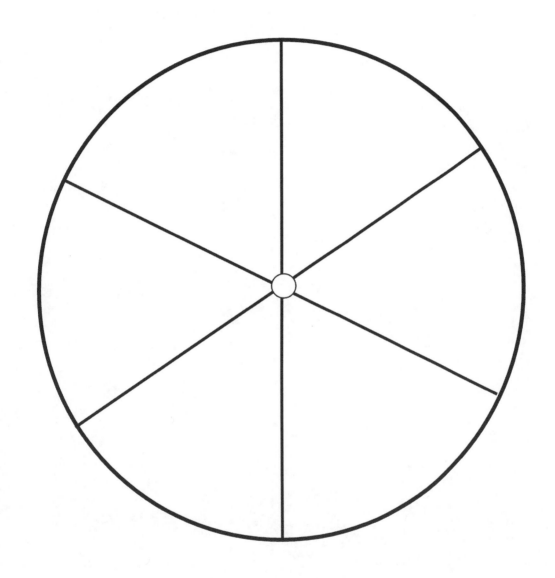

(This page left intentionally blank)

Lapbook Pieces

Cut out the map and the key. Color in the map to show where in the world you can find your animal. Be sure to mark the key.

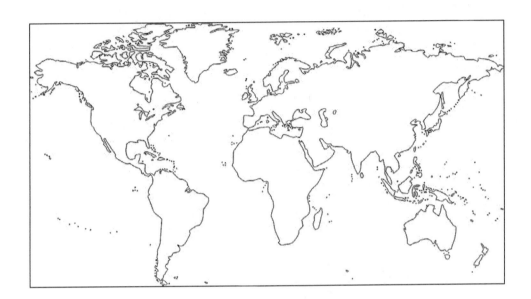

Key

(This page left intentionally blank)

Lapbook Pieces

Cut out the rectangles and fold on the dotted line. Inside (opposite the "glue here" side), write your information. Be sure to add a title and artwork if you desire.

(glue here)

(glue here)

(This page left intentionally blank)

Lapbook Pieces

Cut as one piece and fold the outside squares to cover the middle. Label the piece and add artwork if you'd like.

(This page left intentionally blank)

Experiment Worksheet

Fill out this worksheet as you work through the experiment.

Question: _____

Hypothesis: _____

_____

Materials: _____

_____

Procedure: _____

_____

_____

_____

_____

Observations/data: _____

_____

_____

_____

Conclusion: _____

_____

_____

(This page left intentionally blank)

Research Notes

Use these pages to make notes on your topic.

Topic:_____

Resource 1:_____

Info:_____   Info:_____

Info:_____   Info:_____

Info:_____   Info:_____

Resource 2:_____

Info:_____   Info:_____

Info:_____   Info:_____

Info:_____   Info:_____

Resource 3:_____

Info:_____   Info:_____

Info:_____   Info:_____

Info:_____   Info:_____

Resource 4:_____

Info:_____   Info:_____

Info:_____   Info:_____

Info:_____   Info:_____

(This page left intentionally blank)

Resource 5:_____

Info:_____   Info:_____

Info:_____   Info:_____

Info:_____   Info:_____

Resource 6:_____

Info:_____   Info:_____

Info:_____   Info:_____

Info:_____   Info:_____

Resource 7:_____

Info:_____   Info:_____

Info:_____   Info:_____

Info:_____   Info:_____

Resource 8:_____

Info:_____   Info:_____

Info:_____   Info:_____

Info:_____   Info:_____

Resource 9:_____

Info:_____   Info:_____

Info:_____   Info:_____

Info:_____   Info:_____

(This page left intentionally blank)

Science Report Checklist

Use this checklist to help you as you finish up your science project. Aim for a checkmark in each box.

Research
☐ Facts
☐ Sources
☐ Bibliography

Project
☐ 3D
☐ Neat
☐ Teaches all about your topic; shows off all you learned
☐ Self-explanatory: someone could look at it and understand what it's all about without you explaining it to them
☐ Bibliography displayed with project

Experiment
☐ Demonstrates your topic
☐ Neatly written up with all parts of the experiment worksheet
☐ Able to be done over and over with the same results

Demonstration
☐ Clearly state what your project is about
☐ Tell about what they will learn from your project
☐ Explain how the experiment relates to your topic
☐ Demonstrate the experiment
☐ State your conclusion
☐ Ask if anyone has questions

Made in the USA
Columbia, SC
09 August 2024

40211054R00265